THE WHITE EAGLE LODGE STORY

SOME WORDS FROM WHITE EAGLE

'We have far to travel, dear ones; as yet we have only a fragmentary idea of brotherhood; this Lodge must become a family … a great family …and even greater than a family, it must become a brotherhood in spirit and in truth.'
STELLA POLARIS, *February–March 1961*

The White Eagle Lodge Story:

Seventy-Five Years of Work with the Light

Told by friends of
White Eagle across the years

THE WHITE EAGLE PUBLISHING TRUST

NEW LANDS : LISS : HAMPSHIRE : ENGLAND

First published as THE WHITE EAGLE LODGE STORY September 2008
A previous version published as THE STORY OF THE WHITE EAGLE
LODGE, complete to 1986, in October 1986

British Library Cataloguing-in-Publication Data
A catalogue record for this book is available
from the British Library

ISBN 978-0-85487-198-8

ACKNOWLEDGMENTS AND DEDICATION

*In addition to the many contributors to the text of this book, the photographers
are many and various, as are those who have sought out photographs and
references for us and allowed their photographs and research to be used. The
list of those who have helped would be too long to give here in full; instead, we
thank them all – collectively here, but individually in our hearts.*

*So this book is dedicated to all of White Eagle's worldwide family, both
in spirit and on earth, with our love and thanks. White Eagle and the
Brotherhood thank each of you for your service and work for the light, and
every one of you is known and valued as we go forward together, under the Star.
Many of those about whom we have written are now in the world of spirit,
but they are still part of the big White Eagle family: still working with us,
ever more closely, as the bridge of light between the two worlds becomes
stronger through our aspiration and meditation.*

*We remember you all with great affection and we
dedicate this book to you in love and thankfulness.*

*The compilers of this book, who were principally Ylana Hayward
(first edition) and its editors Colum Hayward (both editions) and Sara Cody
(this edition); also Jenny Dent, who wrote the epilogue to this edition.*

Set in Baskerville at the Publisher
and printed in Great Britain by
Cambridge University Press

Contents

Introduction to the Second Edition   7

Introduction to the Original Edition, 1986   8

I.   Burstow and Pembroke Hall   11

II.   The War Years   25

III.   New Lands   41

IV.   The Temple   62

V.   Continuing Minesta's Work   87

VI.   On up the Mountain   98

VII.   A Worldwide Work of Healing   120

VIII.   Uniting under the Star: Renewed Vision   148

        Epilogue   153

SPECIAL PHOTO FEATURES

A UK Daughter Lodge Round-up   72–3

Brothers through the Years   96–7

Golden Jubilee Party and Avebury –New Lands Walk   100–101

In West Africa   130

Additional Notes on the Illustrations   157

Introduction to the Second Edition

The publication of THE STORY OF THE WHITE EAGLE LODGE in 1986 celebrated fifty years of the White Eagle work. It told the compelling story of the origins and development of the worldwide movement that grew out of a small group of people serving Spirit into an international network of brethren and friends, supported by an organisation that has sought to help thousands towards spiritual health, healing and happiness.

In the twenty or so years since the first book was published, the world has changed, and so has the White Eagle work. As the work developed the original book remained popular but left readers wanting more. Now, following much demand, this new edition is published, still telling the story of those first early years – but now covering seventy-five, from the birth of the White Eagle brotherhood to the present day.

Looking over seventy-five years, we see change, and yet constancy.... At the heart of the whole story there always was, and always will be, White Eagle's teaching. It is simple, unique, unchallenged; a pure spiritual guidance; it forms the basis of a philosophy of life that remains as vibrant and practical today as it did at the outset.

Now in the Lodge we move forwards, turning our vision towards a true 'school of the spirit'. In this vision White Eagle has a new face as a spiritual teacher for today, with a practical philosophy for the twenty-first century that combines threads from all the world's religions. As we watch the White Eagle work spreading the world over, within our hearts we are closer than ever before: united in the light of our faith, our purpose, and our love.

In this second edition, the original text has been lightly edited for reasons of consistency and accuracy, but we have avoided editing anything already in quotation. Many of the photographs from 1986 have been retained, but we have tried also to vary the selection. We have also tried to make the book less centred on the Mother Lodge than the 1986 edition, but this is not an easy task when the tree now has so many branches. There is also a slight bias towards recording those who have already 'gone before' over the living. Nonetheless it is the individual, and what many individuals together represent, that we have sought most to honour in this new volume.

Opposite: Minesta (Grace Cooke) as a young woman

Introduction to the Original Edition, 1986

This is the story of an organisation founded at the instigation of a group of brothers in the world of spirit, whom we shall call the brethren of the Great White Light. If it had a subtitle, it would probably be 'guidance, vision, brotherhood', for that defines the relationship between those who do the work on earth and those who direct it in the higher world. The guidance should be evident throughout the book, and also the vision given to them by the brothers above, which the work's earthly leaders have demonstrated. The brotherhood is the ideal which, set before them by the brothers of the Light, the followers of the teaching seek to put into practice, for it is only by the practice of brotherhood that anything at all is created, as far as this work is concerned.

White Eagle is the spokesman for this group of brothers in the world of spirit. He is our teacher, but though he brings with him the gentle personality of an Indian chief, his name simply means a wise teacher, and there are times when it is better not to think of the individual, but of the group above who guide and watch over us.

A detail from the portait of White Eagle by R. Vicaji

White Eagle's medium, for all of her earthly life, was our founder Minesta, Mrs Grace Cooke, now herself in the world of spirit with Brother Faithful (Ivan Cooke, her husband), and like White Eagle very, very active in the guidance of the work at the intuitive level. We call her Minesta in this book, which was the name she had when in an incarnation in the Mayan civilization. That story is told in her book, now called MEMORIES OF REINCARNATION. Brother Faithful is the name White Eagle gave to Ivan Cooke in this life, and it so suits him that we use it here, and ask for the patience of those who would have preferred earthly names to be used, as they read this book. The remarkable story of their coming together has yet to be told.

Minesta's qualities as a leader, her courage and her fidelity to the work she was given to do, will we hope be evident to all who read this book. We of her family, who have compiled it, remember her above all as a mother, and know that the love she showed to each of us was the same as she showed to each of the members of her wider 'family' in the Lodge. As Joan Hodgson, Minesta's eldest daughter, once said,

> 'Above all, White Eagle and the Brotherhood wanted the teaching to remain always simple and pure. He wanted the work to be built on a loving family spirit of helpfulness, kindness and sympathetic understanding of each other's difficulties, not only practical

difficulties, but the soul struggles which beset each one of us according to our karma. Often even her closest family could not understand at the time why Minesta acted in a certain way, or made certain decisions, but we soon learnt to respect these decisions and follow her guidance.... Minesta's "bright eyes", looking into the future, enabled her to foresee the pitfalls likely to arise through the weaknesses in human nature, and guard against them.'

Joan Hodgson, 'Personal Recollections of Minesta and White Eagle', STELLA POLARIS, October–November 1980

Ivan Cooke (Brother Faithful), early 1930s

Brother Faithful spent all his life by Minesta's side, from the time he met her, protecting her and enabling her always to give of her best. His untiring work and the strength of his personality were as important as her own energy in the building of the Lodge as a group of servers, students of the Light, and his wisdom and humour gave it a character all will remember with very great affection. His special contribution (besides being a wonderful healer and sensitive himself) was in getting White Eagle's teaching into print: he was the editor of all the early books and also of ANGELUS, the Lodge magazine, and its successor STELLA POLARIS.*

This book is a rather personal story of the Lodge. Though we hope that friends who have newly been introduced to the teaching will enjoy it, some will take a little time to adjust to the way of looking at life that the book demonstrates. A Lodge is a gatehouse to the mansion which lies beyond, but it is also a place where those on their journey through life may come for refreshment and, in resting, find greater insight. We welcome all who read this book into our Lodge and pray that they may realise the loving acceptance of our teacher.

*In this book you will also meet (we state the relationships here for clarity) Joan's husband John Hodgson and their daughters Rose (who became Rose Elliot) and Jenny (who became Jenny Dent). You will also meet Minesta's younger daughter Ylana, who married Geoffrey Hayward and had twin sons Colum and Jeremy (whose wife Anna you will also meet). The inner family then broadens out to include a vast number of people who have given selflessly to see the organisation – we would far prefer to say the brotherhood – grow. If this book succeeds in presenting a picture of active brotherhood, with many, many named and unnamed individuals all contributing to one great ideal, then it will have done its work.

CHAPTER I

Burstow and Pembroke Hall

THIS WORK was planned a long time ago. You yourselves have been drawn to it by links of karma. Although everyone likes to feel that he or she is wholly independent, actually no soul is wholly free. For it is tied by fine links to its own past, and also to its future. This is how you have all been drawn to this work.

Whenever a small group commences this kind of work the White Brotherhood above watch over it. This happened with the Christian brotherhoods of long ago who also worked unknown and unseen. They persisted bravely and faithfully over the years so that all mankind today has much for which to thank these Christian brothers. They gave their life, their service to humanity. So may it be with you.

White Eagle's address at the Silver Jubilee
Service, London Lodge, 22 February 1961

Fireplace at Burstow Manor

Opposite page: the opening of Burstow on 25 March 1933. On Minesta's right is Estelle Stead; flanking the group are Joan and Ylana. Behind, in the doorway, centre, is W. R. Bradbrook, who took down all the Conan Doyle messages described below, p. 13. Also present, behind Miss Stead, is Frank Wharhirst (see p. 47, 81)

THERE IS really no beginning, and no end. But we have chosen to tell a chapter, and we look back seventy-two years, to 1936. Or rather, we look a few years earlier, for the Lodge was conceived not in Kensington that year, but at Burstow Manor in Surrey, a little previously.

Grace Cooke (White Eagle used to call her 'Brighteyes' and later 'Minesta', the name we shall use in this book) was first introduced to Burstow in 1929, when her help and that of Brother Faithful (Ivan Cooke) was sought by its owner to help in the release of an earthbound soul: 'as sorrowful an earthbound soul as ever I met' – so Brother Faithful later described her. Happiness came out of sorrow: the story of the release of Mary is movingly told by Brother Faithful in THE HEAVENS ARE RINGING (1930). Subsequently Minesta was called there again – this time to help, through her psychic gift, in the search for a 'buried treasure' which Burstow's owner, a Mrs Trotter, had been assured was buried there. Time has revealed that treasure to be of a spiritual rather than an earthly nature; for out of the spiritual contact which was made through that work, and the work with Mary, grew the vision of Burstow as a healing and retreat centre. As far back as 1924 Mrs Trotter had been told from spirit that 'this old house, built in a place of prayer and sanctity, been chosen as the centre for a brotherhood yet to be formed, from which would emanate influence and teaching which would eventually become worldwide'. And in 1929 White Eagle himself had told her that it was a place of spiritual peace, one of the special centres of Britain: 'one for them [the spirit world] to use for the purpose they know of. It is only in this place that the seed can be sown'.

And so it came about that in 1932 Burstow was leased for an initial three years, to be used as a centre for healing and retreat. Just about this time a man and his wife had come to White Eagle in dire need – he was unemployed, with a little family to support – and it was partly to help them that the venture was embarked upon, for they were installed to manage the home, leaving White Eagle's medium free (or so she hoped) to do the spiritual work.

Burstow was a little hamlet, lying just off what was then the Brighton road, about thirty miles from London. Rather as with New Lands today, as soon as one turned off the busy main road into the little lane leading to the old house, with the church by its side, the old rectory, and a few cottages which comprised the hamlet, there was a feeling of remoteness from the world, and a peace. It was almost like going into another age. Part of the house was really old, with massive oak beams and a great fireplace that took enormous logs. You could sit right inside this fireplace next to the fire and roast comfortably; or, if you chose, come out from this inglenook

Burstow Manor

and freeze. The rest was of more recent date with less atmosphere, though more convenient. We remember a vast kitchen range which consumed coal at a great rate – but coal was only thirty shillings a ton then. A path ran round the boundary of the lawn and flower-beds, where with inner vision monks in brown habits, from another age, could be seen, walking as if in prayer. We came to know the gentle presences of Amyas, Clement and Joseph quite well, and called the path 'The Monks' Walk'. Many years later, when our first sight of New Lands was of green lawns bordered by a sheltered walk, we felt at once we had come home to Burstow. It was 'The Monks' Walk' all over again.

From 1929 or before, White Eagle had been speaking about the White Brotherhood (as he then called it) in the world of light, and of how earthly centres of the Brotherhood would be established in various parts of the world. He said that certain men and women, linked consciously or unconsciously with the Lodge of the Brother-hood in the world above, would in due course be drawn together to form the nuclei of groups, drawn together for the purpose of working with the power of good- or God-thought – the power of the Light – for the welfare of humankind, and to bring about the unfoldment of human consciousness.

> If there could come a unification of these men and women of goodwill, their formation into Groups or Lodges [White Eagle in-dicated], then, instead of individual contact with the light, would be that more powerful thing, a collective reception. Such groups in turn would then serve as distributors for the Light – that great White Light which at the Source is the very breath and being of Christ … and to such service his medium and others might find themselves called, albeit in humble capacity.
>
> *Ivan Cooke,* THE WHITE BROTHERHOOD

In these early years, confirmation of the existence of the Brother-hood in the world of spirit came too from a completely separate source. There was published at the end of 1929 a book entitled MAN MADE PERFECT, which consisted of teachings received from the White Brotherhood through the hand of Mabel Beatty. The teach-ings contained in the book and those given by White Eagle were so similar that Minesta was invited to join Mrs Beatty's group, and she attended regularly in 1930–31. White Eagle spoke within this group from time to time, and so did Brother Faithful's guide, 'Friend'.

On 27 January 1931, at a small gathering in Westminster arranged by the Polaire Brotherhood of Paris and the Conan Doyle family, Sir Arthur Conan Doyle spoke through Minesta for the first time. The Polaires had formed in 1929, and their teaching was that of true brotherhood through the realisation of the spirit within. The Polaires' instructions in instigating the January gathering were received through a mathematical means of divination, and were remarkable in the extent to which they corresponded with what was being received mediumistically in England regarding the work of the White Brotherhood. Following White Eagle's guidance, Minesta and Brother Faithful were initiated into the Brotherhood in Paris later in 1931. It was not until February 1934 – after much testing in the area of human relationships, and what Minesta was later to describe as 'the deepest spiritual suffering' (STELLA POLARIS, 1963), testing which caused the temporary closure of the home Burstow – that definite instructions were received from the Brotherhood above that a Lodge of the Polaires was to be formed there. An emissary came from Paris to assist in the formation of this group, which met regularly from the summer of that year onwards.

Polaire Bulletin, October 1931, noting an article 'Conan Doyle et les Polaires'

A word now about those who gathered to hear White Eagle at Burstow in those days. In the early 1930s, the teacher was becoming known and loved by an increasing number of people through his talks to audiences at the Marylebone Spiritualist Association (now the S.A.G.B.); at the London Spiritual Mission in Pembridge Place (founded by Ernest and Percy Beard – to whose son, Paul, we shall refer later); and at the W. T. Stead Library and Bureau in Westminster. Here White Eagle's medium worked with and for W. T. Stead's daughter, Estelle, and gave much remarkable evidence and comfort and guidance to those who came privately for help. The publication of the messages from Sir Arthur in the book THY KINGDOM COME also served to focus attention on the work at Burstow. Subsequently Estelle Stead became one of the Burstow brothers, and was on the platform at the opening of the Lodge in 1936. It was from these contacts that the little group gathered round the Cooke family were drawn – in addition, of course, to those living locally who attended the Sunday services at the Manor.

Minesta at Burstow with an early Brother, 'Mauris' (Anne Bowen)

The original core of brothers (men and women) numbered just twelve. They met every week at Burstow and sometimes at the Stead Library as well. But the group grew fast: by the end of the first year, 1934, there were nearly thirty of them; and by the end of 1935, over fifty (including a group who met in Edinburgh, as we shall see). We remember many of these early brothers with special affection: their service was not necessarily greater than those who have come after, but their significance is great, and those who are no longer with us on earth today surely work with us from the other side of life, giving their support still to the work of the Brotherhood.

Brother Faithful describes Burstow in THE HEAVENS ARE RINGING as 'a wonderful old place of great oaken beams, of quaint passages and flights of unexpected stairs, and windows opening to views of lawns and lake or green-clad trees'. We remember vividly the chorus of nightingales through warm May nights, and the glow-

Three of the brothers initiated in 1934: Blue Star (Mrs C. Malcolm); Christian (Ylana, then known normally as Greta Cooke; and Ray (Lady Doris Segrave)

worms which picked out the path for us with their bright gleam. The chief 'view of lawns and lake' was from an upper room that had been a billiard- and play-room but was now transformed into a chapel, that chapel which will always be remembered because it was there that the first seeds of the Brotherhood work were sown.

The Brethren will not forget the little chapel. Chilly or overheated, exuberantly draughty or sweltering under the sun, in memory it stands out as wholly beautiful, gracious, wholly peaceful. We remember the lilies upon the altar, the soft lights above, the seated circle of the Brethren. Outside perhaps it was a summer's night, and dusk was gathering; there would come the scent of trodden grass, of flowers, the hush of nature wherein are interwoven multitudinous sounds of breathings, yet which holds in itself a silence profound. It was then as if the Brethren were joined in an at-one-ment with all creation – with grass and flower, bush and tree, bird and beast, with the soft night winds and starlight. Then, indeed, the Brotherhood embraced all living things – and reached out and found very close and real those mystical and magical powers which encompassed us.

Ivan Cooke, in THE WHITE BROTHERHOOD

Early in 1935 came another period of spiritual trials and human difficulties, as a result of which the English Brotherhood became completely independent of the French group. The significance of this is considerable, for with the coming of the Second World War and the 'years of fire' so long predicted by the Wise Ones, and in particular the occupation of Paris by the German army, the visible group in Paris was no longer able to operate. It seems to us, looking back, that there was a gradual transmission of spiritual energy from the original Polaire group to the Brotherhood in England. The latter was able to work without hindrance throughout the war years, unlike its parent; and maybe only because of a very visible break which had taken place. After the break with the French group the name of the English one was changed, under White Eagle's guidance, to the White Brotherhood and (later) the Star Brotherhood.

The time at Burstow was a deeply testing one for everyone – there were manifold difficulties and much pain, as well as great happiness and remarkable spiritual illumination. It turned out to be a training ground where much was learnt and much experience gained. Looking back on the problems, one gets the overall impression that they all had a very definite purpose. The regular association with the Polaire Brotherhood was apparently not meant to last, but it brought the little English Brotherhood under the strong Polaire Star. The vicissitudes in the administration of Burstow caused the running of the Brotherhood (and later the Lodge) to be brought entirely under spiritual guidance, not the guidance of any earthly committee or council. Further, the tests and trials rallied the faithful to the centre of the work. And at the earthly level much was learnt about the practical running of a spiritual centre.

When the lease on Burstow expired in the autumn of 1935 it was believed that the Brotherhood would be able to buy the house. Such were the earthly hopes, but they were soon to be dashed. Painful it was, once more, and yet White Eagle was already guiding our thoughts towards the London centre. 'First the London centre, then the country home…' he said prophetically (although Burstow was of course the birthplace). It was a surprising direction, yet intrinsic to the Lodge's growth. As to Burstow: it is now a mile from Gatwick Airport, and right under the take-off path. Maybe not such an ideal place for meditation activities today!

Atar at Burstow Manor

> When the time came to leave the Manor House – rather a saddening task – the chapel was dismantled; and strange it was to note how even prior to that dismantling the power and sanctity seemed to fade away. At the last meeting of the Brotherhood it was, as ever, its sanctuary and shrine; it became no more than any other room when stripped, and that which had sanctified it was withdrawn into the invisible.
>
> Then followed a difficult time. We had been instructed to seek premises in town, and what was needed seemed almost unattainable. Many months expired, during which some few of the Brethren held their Lodge in the home of two of the Brethren, which meetings served to keep the flame alight.
>
> *Ivan Cooke, in* THE WHITE BROTHERHOOD

The two were Hilda and James Pritchard, known in the Brotherhood as 'Ruth' and 'James'. We name them, and with great love, because they were later to become truly pillars of the Lodge, and their contribution to White Eagle's work in service at all levels is incalculable. Their daughter, Mary Yoxall, was active in her attendance at the Brotherhood when she passed on in 1998.

Then at last we heard of premises in Kensington.

Sister 'Mary' Yoxall, initiated 1935

> That White Eagle guided us to the premises is literally true; because after we had spent some months looking for the desired accommodation he quietly sent a message advising us to go without delay to the house agent (the agent was specified) to enquire for vacant premises. Having learnt by this time to act on this inner voice, we lost no time. Sure enough, the house agent had, only an hour before we arrived, received notification that Pembroke Hall, Kensington, had become vacant and could be leased at a suitable rental. On inspecting the premises, we found ourselves somewhat dismayed. The property was in a bad condition, re-

quiring rather extensive repairs and redecoration throughout. However, as these were the premises indicated for the future activities of White Eagle and his group of the White Brotherhood, we accepted the position as inevitable and proceeded to make preparations for the opening.

Grace Cooke, in PLUMED SERPENT

The lease was signed on 20 January, and Pembroke Hall, redecorated and furnished, was dedicated and opened, under the name of The White Eagle Lodge, on 22 February 1936. It seems incredible, looking back, when we realise how much was accomplished in those few short weeks, and it is a tribute to Minesta's ever-creative vision that she was able from the start to see not what the place was but what it could be, the friendly and beautiful home for the White Eagle work which the public first saw on that great day. It was a tribute also to the devotion and industry of the little group from the time at Burstow who stood firm after the closure and gave unstinted help in this great new venture.

White Eagle has always taught that workers for the spirit had also to be prepared to get down on their knees and scrub the floor of their Lodge, and this we now found ourselves doing. Brother Faithful built the platform, altar and reading desks with his own hands.

Main Chapel, Pembroke Hall

As well as the main chapel, there was a small chapel where later all the early 'inner teachings' were to be given.

The altar, and other furnishings from the Manor House chapel, served to make a smaller chapel, as nearly as possible a replica, and it was remarkable how the power and sanctity of the former chapel seemed to return.

Ivan Cooke, in THE WHITE BROTHERHOOD

Brotherhood Chapel,
Pembroke Hall

On the opening day the new chapel, transformed from the somewhat seedy dance-hall, was filled to capacity; and sharing the platform with Minesta and Brother Faithful were Estelle Stead and Shaw Desmond, well-known figures in the Spiritualist Movement. The last-named, with a flash of insight, referred to the Lodge as a lighthouse in the dark world, a theme which White Eagle took up in his address. Later, that symbol of the lighthouse was going to mean a great deal. We quote now from White Eagle's dedication of the Lodge:

We have chosen to call this centre the White Eagle Lodge – a name not bearing reference to any particular person but referring to the white eagle as a symbol of vision, used down the ages by the Wise Ones whom we are privileged to serve.

This is to be a centre of light; and all who would serve the Great White Light, whatever their denomination, whatever their school of thought, can meet here on a common plane of brotherhood and service.

Therefore, beloved children, we say that this place is to be a lighthouse to guide men and women, and we ask you to help us establish and maintain the light within. Let this become a focal point for the light of spirit.

Unite with us in spirit so that we may be at one with the Christ Light.

Now we would ask you to be absolutely still within; to put aside all worldly cares and thoughts, to be ready and open and so contact the great Light which is now pouring down upon us all. ...

In the name of God we call upon the Angels of Light, of Wisdom and of Power, to bless, sanctify and dedicate this centre to the service of Christ. May those who minister herein heal the sick and comfort those who mourn; may they remove the blindfold from the eyes of those who see not, and give hearing to those who are deaf; may they at all times give forth from their hearts and lives the love of God, bringing peace on earth, helping to establish brotherhood between men and harmony between nations.

So be it.

In the words of the Master we say: *Feed my sheep* – in daily service and love.

Pembroke Hall stood at the meeting of five roads, and if you were to go today and stand where the old Lodge stood you might wonder how a quiet work of prayer and communion and spiritual healing and teaching could ever be accomplished or even contemplated there. Well, it was quieter then; not quite the rush and roar of traffic that there is today. But more than this, a seven-foot solid brick wall stood between us and the road* and once through the narrow gate into the little courtyard beyond you were in a new and quieter world. And you would go straight forward through what must at one time have been a small conservatory – for it was all glass – into the main chapel, which seated about a hundred and fifty people and was quiet and peaceful with its blue curtains, white walls and the simple altar adorned with the fragrant *Longii* lilies, the weekly gift of one kind member.

The conservatory (swelteringly hot in summer of course) was an excellent vestibule for the main chapel. On the left was a tiny room not much more than four by five feet, which was Brother Faithful's office. Here he did all his writing in those early days – he was a prolific writer – and from here he would emerge benign and humorous to greet and talk to visitors and take new patients under his wing (for in those very early days he was our chief and only healer). This little room also housed the first White Eagle Lodge library (it must have had expanding walls). On the right of the vestibule was the secretary's office, slightly bigger but not much so, though it was a pleasant little room with a window looking out onto the courtyard and an escape route through the main chapel which the harassed secretary sometimes found very useful!

Members' Room, Pembroke Hall

If you preferred, instead of going forward into the main chapel you could turn left as you entered the courtyard, and walk round the building into a quiet little paved garden sheltering under a plane tree; and from the garden you would pass into a small cottage. Fairly elderly and somewhat cramped it was, but never mind! It served to provide a meeting room and cloakroom for members. Then there was a small kitchen in which the member was greeted by a little old-fashioned lady clad in spotless white apron and wearing high-buttoned boots, who provided tea and delicious thin bread and butter. She was always known as Mrs Button-Boots.

Upstairs was a room of which gracious and lovely memories remain, for this was 'White Eagle's room' where all the early

*The 1986 edition comments that there is still a wall there today. In 2008, this remains true, but the site appears now to be being redeveloped, after remaining an empty space (see page 30) for thirty-one years)

spiritual unfoldment groups took place, the room where the first instruction in meditation was given (it was then a little-known art in the West), and the room to which many a soul came seeking comfort in their grief or need, and so often emerged – radiant and transformed after a private hour with White Eagle. In this room also, Minesta had the memorable contact (described in THE SHINING PRESENCE) with the Master from India, which had a profound effect upon her.

This room lay directly above the Members' Room, and it was all the inevitable chatter below that led Brother Faithful to indite his memorable notice to those using the room: 'Please keep your conversation low'! A narrow passage divided this room from the two small healing chapels, partitioned off in those few short weeks between the signing of the lease and the opening day: and from this passage a way had been cut through the thick wall to the balcony over the main chapel. It was a very small opening, resulting in many a bruised head. We guessed it was to teach us humility!

We have described Pembroke Hall in some detail, feeling that these early beginnings will be of special interest to all our friends and family. It will be seen how perfectly adapted was this whole building to the then needs of the Lodge, and how true had been White Eagle's guidance in leading us there.

White Eagle's Room, Pembroke Hall. A note on a copy of this photograph says it was taken by early Brother Anne Bowen (Mauris)

After the opening came the period of building. Looking back on those early days it is difficult to imagine how Minesta and Brother Faithful managed to sustain single-handed, with a secretarial staff of one [Ylana – who was Minesta's younger daughter – though with wonderful voluntary help], the programme of activities they set themselves, but both were full of enthusiasm and a burning desire to help humanity, and seemed to be carried along by a spiritual power far greater than their own. They certainly needed it, for as well as two public services each week, there was a weekly Inner Teaching by White Eagle as well as many private appointments for healing, guidance and consolation.

All the public services were conducted by Minesta and Brother Faithful, both of whom were experienced in public work. Minesta was a superb clairvoyant and when the White Eagle Lodge was first opened she would give clairvoyance at all the public meetings except when White Eagle was speaking, for she felt that this was a way of drawing enquirers and support to the Lodge.

Joan Hodgson, 'Personal Recollections of Minesta and White Eagle', STELLA POLARIS, June–July 1980

From small beginnings the work at Pembroke Hall grew and flourished. It was a great act of faith, for its founders had no capital behind them on which to run the Lodge, and were extremely dependent on the goodwill of White Eagle followers and the hard work of those involved. Friends were invited to support the Lodge by becoming Members, and we still remember the very first person to walk into the little office and pay her subscription – one guinea then (even the measure, which was one pound one shilling, seems quaint now!). Her name was Edith Quinlan, and she became a good friend and faithful worker. It was she who very shortly afterwards introduced to the Lodge the 'grey-haired stranger' who became our first organist. The original number of members was a hundred and twenty, a number that slowly but very surely grew. The goodwill has never been lacking; nor has the faith that if those most closely involved really served and gave from their hearts, all material needs would be met. That faith has always been justified, though it must be confessed that there have been anxious moments!

White Eagle had already spoken at Burstow about a new method of spiritual healing through light rays. This form of healing was to form an important part of the work in the future. It was shortly after the opening of the Lodge that he directed us to form the absent healing groups that have become such a feature of the White Eagle path. Healers were trained under his guidance, and the new method of the mental and spiritual projection of coloured light rays, in co-operation with the angels of healing, about which we were beginning to learn, got under way. At first there were just two groups, gradually increasing to the five that were working at the time war broke out in 1939.

Another event which had a great effect on the future of the work was the appearance, in duplicated form, of a monthly Lodge magazine – ANGELUS – in response to direct guidance, even as to the name itself, given to Minesta. ANGELUS offered us a chance to keep in touch with our small band of members and to help draw them together as a family – as STELLA POLARIS does today. The name was intended to give the feeling of the 'call to prayer'. Soon we could read:

The first issue of ANGELUS has been kindly received. Its readers have overlooked shortcomings, praised any merits, and translated their kindliness into action by either passing on their own copy, or obtaining further copies for their friends, ANGELUS and its staff anticipated no less.

Do not, however, enquire of the editorial staff (comprising one person) why the first issue of ANGELUS was duplicated and not printed. Do not stress the many advantages of printing over duplicating. The staff will only respond with a pallid smile. It knows the answer. Do not repeat your question in our duplicating, binding and despatching Works (the Works measuring six feet by eight, and staffed by two persons). They have turned the handle of the

The very first issue of ANGELUS

duplicator many thousands of times; sorted, arranged and bound so many of the sheets! they know, also – none better. Why rouse them to frenzy, or send them into a decline?

Nevertheless, ANGELUS, made beautiful and more perfect, will, in due course, go out into the world in printed form and thus carry its message to the many instead of the few.

Ivan Cooke in ANGELUS, *July 1936*

It was a promise that was eventually made good, as we shall see.

In 1937 we published the first-ever book of White Eagle's teaching, ILLUMINATION. It consisted of talks he gave before the opening of the Lodge, at various Spiritualist services in London. Handsomely printed on paper with uncut edges, it was illustrated with woodcuts and bound in stiff board covers and sold for two shillings. We shall never forget the thrill of opening the first batch of books the printers delivered. The smell of the ink lingers, amid many memories of that great moment. How splendid our previously empty bookstall looked once the new books were on display!*

ILLUMINATION immediately won new friends to the Lodge, one of whom was none other than our dear John Hodgson, later Joan's husband.† Another whom it brought in that year was a young man who many years later was to become our legal adviser: Noel Gabriel. So we owe that book quite a lot. Looking at our records, 1938 always seems a very rich year in terms of our growing community. This period also saw another come into the Lodge whose gifts were to be greatly valued later: Teddy Dent, the author of the two poems reproduced in the book MEDITATION, and the father of Geoffrey Dent. (We shall meet them again on p. 39).

The first book was followed after six months by another, ways of service in the world today, consisting of inner teachings given in the new Lodge; and later in 1938 came THE CHRISTIAN MYSTERIES, another set of recent inner teachings (interpreting, largely, the Revelation of St John). The newly-formed 'White Eagle Publications' thus succeeded in publishing three books in sixteen months, no mean achievement. These three and ANGELUS, together with the regular distribution of the White Eagle inner teachings in duplicated form, established the White Eagle Lodge in the love and respect of a following which soon extended beyond the shores of this country.

We read in ANGELUS, for instance, of 'a large order for copies of ILLUMINATION for New York'. We have happy memories of the great effort each week to transcribe, type, duplicate and assemble copies of the inner teachings ready for sale the week after they were given. Our two gallant helpers in this task were still with us at our Golden Jubilee. One of them, Leonard Willis, Brother 'Steadfast',

*A facsimile edition of this book was produced for Brothers in 2007.
†see middle photograph, and again below, p. 36.

Opposite page: the first major collection of White Eagle's teaching, ILLUMINATION; John Hodgson, Brother Johannes, and Brother Steadfast (Leonard Willis)

Reginald Botcherby (Brother John)

David Burn-Callander (Brother David)

was very much involved in the running of the London Lodge up to his passing in 1997 and thus worked for White Eagle for sixty years. They used to rush to the Lodge from work in order to help with the assembly and stapling of the pages so that the customer had them 'hot from the press'.

Another whom we remember with very deep affection from this period is our organist, Reginald Botcherby, who became Brother 'John': he has just been referred to as the 'grey-haired stranger':

> When he first came the Lodge had been opened for just four weeks and White Eagle was appealing for the beautiful music which he said was essential to the work. By the end of April our grey-haired stranger was playing the organ at a Sunday service and he was subsequently to transform the musical scene which he had found…. Probably few realise with what care he built the musical structure of the services so that there should be no jarring note…. We must refer to his work with the choir which he formed – a prolonged but triumphant struggle against a dearth of tenors and basses, against black-out and bombs.
>
> *Obituary,* ANGELUS, *March 1945*

*

Anyone who examines the early publications will see that they were available not only from Pembroke Hall but also from 'the Scottish branch of the Lodge', 8 Rosebery Crescent, Edinburgh. This 'branch' was to play an important part in the Lodge history, but its beginnings are even more remarkable; they are indeed a vital part of this story.

It was just a few months after the English group of the Brotherhood formed that the Scottish one began. The group's leader, David Burn-Callander, had just returned from Fanning Island, in the remote Pacific, when he first met Minesta. On the island he had received a message through another's mediumship. Minesta writes:

> The message purported to come from a spirit, who said he was working to establish groups of White Brothers on the earth. The spirit went on to say that [Major Burn-Callander] would leave Fanning Island and return to Edinburgh; there he would meet a certain Mrs Cooke, through whom he would be guided to his future work in connection with a Brotherhood. Up to this point [he] had not heard my name and quite simply asked me if I had ever come across a Mrs. Cooke in the course of my travels. To our mutual amusement, I confessed that my name happened to be Cooke.
>
> *Grace Cooke, in* PLUMED SERPENT

Later, White Eagle spoke to the young man through Minesta and told him, as further confirmation, the name under which he had manifested on Fanning Island. The Edinburgh group thus began under White Eagle's clearest instructions.

The Scottish national daily, *The Scotsman*, told its readers on October 2nd:

> THE aims, ideals and work of the "White Brotherhood" were explained by Grace and Ivan Cooke in a lecture given at Edinburgh Psychic College on Tuesday night last week (October 1st).... The Edinburgh group of the White Brotherhood, it was stated, was founded about six months ago. The badge of membership is a six-pointed star.

By 1938 there were eighteen initiated brothers in Edinburgh, and the work of absent and contact healing as well as the Brotherhood work for peace closely mirrored that of the Lodge in London. In July 1939 an announcement in ANGELUS stated:

For about five years there has been a branch of the Brotherhood in [Edinburgh], which for some time past has been outgrowing its premises. The opening of a White Eagle Lodge to house the Brotherhood in Edinburgh is therefore a logical outcome.

A date was set for it, 6 October.

In the event, things did not quite work out as planned for, as the September ANGELUS went to press with the announcement, war broke out. Yet the opening of the Edinburgh Lodge, when it did come, was to play a vital part in the Lodge story.

Margaret Stedman, Sister Pearl, another of the very early leaders of the Edinburgh Lodge, and the mother of Jean Stedman, who lived the last years of her life at New Lands

CHAPTER II

The War Years

*Pen-and-ink drawing by
Selwyn Dunn in the book*
THE WHITE BROTHERHOOD
(see p. 27)

WHEN WAR came, it was the dashing of many, many hopes and the seeming frustration of months, indeed years, of work for the Light, for peace, by the Brotherhood. Moreover, it appeared to call White Eagle's authority into question, for he had said repeatedly that he did not foresee war. For instance, in a remarkable interview with the editor of PSYCHIC NEWS given in 1938 just before Neville Chamberlain despatched the telegram to Hitler that resulted in their Munich meeting, he said:

> I foresee a period of peace.… I do not think there will be a war. I think the war clouds will pass away. But mankind is passing through a tremendous struggle, not only on earth but on the spiritual planes of his being. There are two forces at work, the destructive and the constructive. If man persists in his fears, he is helping to bring about the very thing that he fears.
>
> THE WHITE BROTHERHOOD

In his prophecy White Eagle was not alone: his brother guides in the Spiritualist movement and in occultism said just the same, then and after. A year later it was difficult to comprehend how they could have prophesied peace. War was declared on 3 September 1939, and it seemed to discredit what the guides had said. White Eagle acknowledged this in a talk a week later:

> There has been a great question among Spiritualists as to why the message that there will be no war was given through so many mediums, through so many occult channels. The message was decreed by the Great Lords.… We in the beyond do not question those in a higher position.… Man's criticism and condemnation, if our work proved an apparent failure, was not our concern. Our one aim was to help to keep hope alive in as many hearts as possible for once hope had died the channel for spiritual light and power became closed.
>
> Fear is the weak spot in us all, and this fear abiding in the hearts of humanity had to be counteracted, even to the last possible moment.… Without confidence and hope the Forces of Light could no longer hold the fort against the enemy.…

There will be a sudden cessation of hostilities. God is omnipotent. So far and no farther can man go. Man's freewill is encompassed by the will of God, and God's hand will be stretched forth at the appointed hour, when lessons have been learnt, and 'halt' will be called....

We see joy and rejoicing, we see a glorious peace as the outcome, a rapid growth of brotherhood on earth. Already the brotherhood is being born. Birth pangs must always be painful. God will not test you beyond your strength and even through these troublous days you will find compensation.

White Eagle's address on 10 September 1939,
reprinted in ANGELUS, *October 1939*

Pembroke Hall altar,
customarily adorned with lilies

There are few people today who lived through the years before the declaration of war, and the rest will need to imagine how fear and anticipation built up as the various European crises came and were succeeded by the next. During this whole period White Eagle, in company with other spiritual teachers, constantly encouraged his followers to think positively: to hold the thought that there would be no war; to radiate light to balance and dissipate the forces of darkness. Otherwise, they would be unprotected against the forces that were massing for the great conflict, the 'years of fire' so long predicted by the White Brotherhood in spirit, both to the Polaires and the early English White Eagle group. During the crisis in 1938 Brotherhood groups in the Lodge had been meeting every three hours to work on the inner planes for peace. The intensity of the work comes across clearly in the book the white brotherhood, completed just at the moment war was declared. We recall clearly the continual effort to hold fast to the thought of the Star, radiating light and peace; and to remain steady and peaceful. It was not easy, because one was fighting natural personal fears of the unknown, and constantly being battered by the radio news bulletins and the dire headlines which shouted from every newspaper.

The outbreak of war in September 1939 dealt a shattering blow to the ordered lives of those who worked at, or regularly worshipped in, the Lodge.... Spiritual truths and spiritual wisdom appeared to be at a discount. All the prophecies of the spirit guides had apparently proved failures; for here we were, plunged into war and entering one of the darkest periods in the dreadful history of war....

On the outer plane it seemed a challenge from the forces of materialism to the forces of Light. On the inner, I felt that the spiritual structure of the Lodge was assailed by the enormous waves of materialism and pessimism. The work stood fast, however, unshaken in its purpose – a purpose which with the passing days seemed more and more essential, for without the Lodge many of our followers would have been bereft indeed. Here it is interesting to note that one with clairvoyant vision had seen the Lodge as an oasis of light in a spiritually darkened city.

Grace Cooke, in PLUMED SERPENT

In retrospect, then, it is remarkable how unshaken the Lodge was by the apparent counteraction of the 'no-war prophecies'; and this in turn is an indication of how far White Eagle's following understood the deeper meaning and purpose of his work, rather than the literal words. This must partly be because White Eagle himself stood so firm, as his words on 10 September 1939 indicate. In fact, some of White Eagle's most important teaching was given during these years; and he guided the Brotherhood's work with remarkable detail all through the period of conflict, on many occasions showing extraordinary knowledge of future events. The Brotherhood was formed to help humanity through 'the years of fire' – there was never any doubt about 'years of fire' occurring – and so when these years took the form of world war, the brothers knew their work and they continued with it.

Yet as most readers know, the declaration of war was followed by what became known as the 'phoney' war, when nothing much seemed to be happening.

After those first few weeks of chaos, the work of the Lodge returned close to normal except that the black-out made late evening services impossible, and during the war years the Sunday services in winter were always held in the afternoons. Following the instructions of White Eagle, the devoted band of workers who remained still strove to maintain the Lodge as a centre of peace, love and brotherhood, a place set apart from the fevers of war. The spiritual light was sent forth into the warring world at every third hour of the day.

*Joan Hodgson and Ylana Hayward,
in* BY WHAT AUTHORITY? *(1953)*

*Christmas Tree in
Pembroke Hall, 1938*

The book THE WHITE BROTHERHOOD was published in November 1939, held up for a couple of months by the declaration of war. It had been written to draw more workers into the chains for peace, and thus its publication, when war had been declared, was an act of courage. Yet it was needed more than ever.

*

In the November ANGELUS that year the editor proudly proclaimed: 'Beginning with the December issue, the Christmas number, our journal will be printed'. And he was able to write in January 1940: 'The reception given to the Christmas has been extraordinarily kind – but this we never doubted.... We do ask our readers to add their efforts to ours by passing on their copy of ANGELUS and so cooperating with us.... The blacker the blackout, the greater the need for spiritual illumination in these days.' Later we read that the Christmas issue fell short of the requirements by some hundreds of copies – so it can be seen that the printed ANGELUS got off to a good start and never looked back.

Thus was redeemed the promise to which we referred earlier. Three months later, in March 1940, another hope was realised, for the Edinburgh Lodge was indeed opened and dedicated by White Eagle on the 30th of that month – an event again reported and described by no less august a voice than that of the *Scotsman*.

In July 1940, just before the onset of the Blitz, came a stirring call to service from White Eagle, in an address subsequently entitled 'Let there be Light'. In the course of the address he spoke of 'principalities and powers' and of 'darkness in high places', of the balance between the forces of light and darkness, and of our responsibility and power to help, of how the advance of darkness could be halted by the light.

Title page of the first printed ANGELUS

By adopting a positive attitude, by recognising only the power of the Divine Spirit, and by breathing into your being, morning, noon and night, the Spirit of Christ; by visualising in the mind of your heart the perfect, the gentle, the divine Man, you will create in your aura a light sufficient to reinforce your weaker brethren....

Think, my brethren, what the effect would be if millions in your country were thus radiating light! Think what the effect would be if men abandoned thoughts of self, desire for accumulation or protection for self, and held fast to one dominating thought of peace and brotherhood, and to help men and women to the way of Christ! Will you make this effort? For we tell you that the hosts of heaven are ready and waiting to help humanity.

This spirit of the Light of Christ will save humankind, and this spirit alone....

We pray that everyone hearing our words will be touched, and make a supreme effort, and ... become receptive to the Divine Light of Christ! Send it forth again and again, so that your country, this mystic isle, shall appear in the etheric world as a blazing Cross of Light which no power of darkness can harm....

Were a picture of the Cross of Light displayed on many buildings, in many places . . . the continual beholding of such a sign of power would create a ring of defence around this isle. May this Cross become a living symbol, cleansing the nation of

Main Chapel and Healing Chapel at Hanover Street, Edinburgh

hatred or desire for vengeance, protecting and saving the people.... Your work must not be stayed for one instant. Put on the whole armour of God. Be filled with the power of the Spirit of Christ.... Go forward in this spiritual battle.

Address of 7 July 1940, reprinted as a leaflet

It was as a direct result of this message from White Eagle that the famous 'Cross of Light' poster campaign was launched. Minesta herself describes it here:

A message was received from the beyond that the White Brotherhood wished to have a special poster printed, showing a sleeping city, and above, in the night sky, a large illumined cross with rays of light from it radiating a protective influence over the city.... The circle of light was symbolic of the universal power of God, the rose on the cross signified the potential love of Christ in the hearts of men and women....

The design and preparation of this poster occupied some weeks, it being completed early in August 1940. It will be noted how accurately the beyond anticipated the arrival of the blitzkrieg. Each poster was blessed before being sent out. In other words, in a Brotherhood group the spiritual light was focused upon the posters so that henceforth they became centres of spiritual power. Many thousands of these posters were distributed. They were to be seen, during the worst months of the bombardment suffered by London, on every Underground and Tube station (in which many thousands of people nightly took shelter), displayed on hoardings, on church doors, in factories and in shops all over England and Scotland.

Grace Cooke, in PLUMED SERPENT

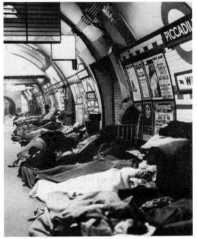

The 'Cross of Light' poster and an Underground station platform with sleeping forms; the poster is visible just right of centre.

The posters are remembered today by persons who knew nothing of the Lodge but found protection and strength from them. We had many letters from people relating how many houses displaying the posters had been undamaged when neighbouring buildings had taken the full force of bomb blast. One woman wrote to say that, carrying the poster, she was untouched by a bomb that fell only a few feet away. Perhaps more important than this, however, was the power the displayed poster had of focusing the forces of Light, of lifting people above the level of fear. As the Battle of Britain reached its height at the beginning of September 1940, the control of the cloud of fear must have been very important to those in the beyond who were working to save humanity. The poster was to be a great source of strength to all of us in the Lodge that autumn....

*

The first Sunday in September was the opening of the Autumn Session. White Eagle gave the address and concluded by making a most unusual request. He said that the Wise Ones requested us to prepare for a special Service of Communion on the following Sunday. Such a Service had never been held before in the Lodge. Arrangements previously made as to speakers, etc., had to be cancelled....

Those who attended this Service of Communion are little likely to forget it....

At the conclusion of the Sacrament [received, as in Lodge services today, in meditation], White Eagle stepped from the rostrum and walked down the aisle for the whole length of the hall, blessing all in the assembly. When he returned to the platform he uttered the last words he ever spoke in that hall.

Grace Cooke, PLUMED SERPENT

These were the closing words:

In the Name of our Lord and King Who is the Christ, we pray ... Father, forgive them, for they know not what they do....

May the peace of the Holy Spirit bless you and keep you safe in His love, now and always. Amen.

And now, the angels will minister to you. Christ's Angels will minister to each one of you; and you may likewise minister on earth to your fellow men in the days to come.

ANGELUS, October 1940

That service was on Sunday 8 September. On the night of Thursday 12 September Pembroke Hall was hit by a bomb and was destroyed.

We may be permitted to dwell on some personal recollections at this point. Joan (Cooke, later Hodgson), who had continued her job as a schoolteacher in the first twelve months of the War and had been evacuated to the country, recalls:

After the first panic at the outbreak of war was over I had been drafted back to London, and at first had to walk round the streets gathering groups of children together and trying to find places where we could give them some lessons and keep them out of mischief. Gradually the empty schools had reopened, not in their old form but with an odd selection of staff who returned from being evacuated; and somehow we all worked together under the guidance of the most senior member. Thus it was that at the time when the blitz started I found myself teaching in a school near Barnes Common [south of the river, maybe five miles from Kensington]. And whenever the air-raid siren went we trooped out with all the children into prepared trenches on the common.

It was after one of those afternoons spent with the children in a trench that the rest of the family picked me up for the journey back to Kent after they had discovered Pembroke Hall in ruins. Although they were full of this dire news, they were unable to pour out the story because we were giving a lift to one of my colleagues!

Ylana writes: 'I remember the extraordinary calm which seemed to grip us when to the sound of wailing sirens announcing yet another raid we arrived to find Pembroke Hall in ruins. Perhaps it was just that it didn't register. I think what really brought us down to earth was when the florist arrived with the usual lilies for the altar for the next Sunday service. It was rather like laying a wreath on the grave!'.

The remarkable thing, of course, is that no-one was inside the building when it was demolished. This was exceptional, and we must go back to a week earlier.

At Grubb's Farm – the unexpected place of sanctuary that saved the lives of Minesta and family – with another early Brother, 'Sapphire Jewel' (Billie Methven)

One of our members – as a rule unable to attend the Lodge on a Sunday – had an urge to come to that special Service of Communion. She said about herself and her husband: 'I really cannot account for the feeling, but I felt we simply had to come'. After the Service was over, and the congregation was dispersing, this friend came to me and said: 'I have just thought that you and your family might come home with us tonight. It will mean fresh country air and perhaps a good night's rest. Will you come? I hesitated for a few moments; then I heard White Eagle's voice saying: 'Go; yes, go.'

Grace Cooke, in PLUMED SERPENT

White Eagle later instructed the family to stay in the country for a few more days, and thus it was that on the night of 12 September, the night the bomb fell, they were not sleeping in the Lodge as they had been doing, feeling safer there than in their London flat.

The news was given to our members in words which even today we find moving. We quote from the October 1940 ANGELUS.

Our readers will learn with sorrow and regret that Pembroke Hall, which has housed the London Lodge for some four years, was partially demolished one night by a bomb which fell nearby.... Those who have worshipped in the Lodge will grieve with us. The peace and beauty which it enshrined would seem destroyed almost beyond redemption, the work built up with such loving care wantonly shattered.

The above is a first reaction; deeper lies the realisation that the work of the White Eagle Lodge still dwells in the hearts of men;

that one supremely loving heart can still lead and help men.… The White Eagle Lodge is founded in this love and brotherhood, and, we believe, must go forward. What has happened to the building which housed the Lodge cannot destroy the work done. Rather it is an incentive to greater effort in the future, even as humanity has now greater need for such work than ever before.…

As to the future we have high hearts. We shall seek new premises, and a greater and more beautiful White Eagle Lodge will arise from what has been razed.

Ivan Cooke, in ANGELUS, *October 1940*

The magazine went on to print the words of the last Communion Service.

Though the Cooke family had been remarkably preserved, and much of the furniture had surprisingly escaped serious damage, the building had not. 'Why had it been allowed to happen?' was a very human question to ask. White Eagle said: 'You must share the fate of humanity if you would learn to give true help and understanding in such a time of need. Why should you escape the common lot?'.

And, in parting, we trust that faithful brethren will learn not to take too much notice of apparent earthly disasters. Take all changes philosophically and see in them a means to a finer end. Nothing is really disastrous; it is only when the vision is limited that disaster is seen. When the vision extends into the great beyond, the soul sees a Light, and love and wisdom and beauty. You are not left alone. Remember the silent Brethren by your side, they will never forsake you. There is nothing to fear in life – except the enemy of all humankind, which is fear. Overcome this last enemy, and you will have found the secret way into heaven.

White Eagle, in ANGELUS, *October 1940*

So far as Minesta was concerned, the bigger the catastrophe, the greater the courage, and within a few days of the bombing the search was on for new premises. Joan took compassionate leave from her teaching job, and the day after she left it they set forth through the air raids to visit possible buildings. They were led to St Mary Abbots Place, only a quarter of a mile from the old Lodge. On entering what is now the main chapel, Minesta said: 'This is the place. I shall work here'. And she did!

During the months following the bombing, the extraordinary provision of those in the inner world who hold the overall plan of the work became apparent. The new White Eagle Lodge in Edinburgh, dedicated by White Eagle in the previous spring, became home for the work. While negotiations were in hand for the new London building, we were invited by our Scottish friends and broth-

The School of Animal Painting, for which 9 St Mary Abbots Place had been built just before the First World War

ers to make our home with them until Christmas (or until negotiations were completed). This meant that the spiritual work could continue without a break: Sunday services, healing and unfoldment groups, and inner teachings. The publication of angelus continued, though Brother Faithful was to complain gently in its pages: 'The secretarial work of the Lodge (which includes the preparation of this journal) is done partly in Kent, partly in Hampshire and in part in Edinburgh, a factor making neither for efficiency nor convenience'. He added, 'It is a grief also that we cannot have our Annual Christmas Tree at Pembroke Hall, a joyful episode to which we have usually looked forward at this Season'.

He needn't have worried! For a most joyous Christmas service was held in the Edinburgh Lodge, and he later wrote: 'At one corner of the Lodge stood a laden Christmas tree, and a congregation outflowed into an adjoining room. In spirit, atmosphere, and joy it was like a Christmas service at Pembroke Hall ... those Christmas services of happy memories'.

It was as a result of the difficult circumstances that the possibility of 'lone healing' work became apparent. As soon as it was known that we were functioning from Edinburgh, people began to write for healing. To cope with this need, healers with experience in the London Lodge were asked to co-operate by doing their work in their own homes at the normal time of the healing group. All the sitters had a copy of the service and a list of patients. Sometimes several would meet together in someone's home, otherwise they would tune in on their own; and somehow we coped with the growing list of patients. As Joan had just come into the work and had no specific responsibility, it seemed natural that she should take over the organisation of this healing work. (This development, which was outwardly due to force of circumstances, fulfilled a prophecy which White Eagle had made to her in the Burstow days when she was anxious about finding the right teaching post. He said: 'Your guide is watching over you all the time and will not allow you to miss the right opportunity when it comes. You will find yourself teaching children of all ages'.)

Back now to London and the new Lodge! And in January 1941 Brother Faithful prepared readers of ANGELUS for the opening:

We have a new home for a new age, new work to undertake. When you enter our new Lodge (as we hope you will and soon) you may think that here is a simple yet gracious (and spacious) building. For what purpose it was originally built we do not know – an art school, perhaps, or a studio accommodating many students [this was a right assumption, as the photograph opposite shows]. The building is situated in a quiet cul de sac off the Kensington High Street, known as St Mary Abbots Place, from

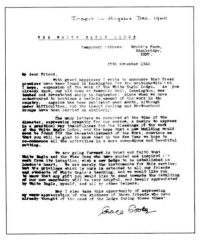

Letter announcing the new premises and reopening

which a door opens to a paved court, across which an entrance flanked on either side by pillars admits one to the main hall, a portion of which is raised as for a stage (here can be presented the mystical plays we have planned, and even commenced to produce last year). The hall has walls of white, a floor covered with white rubber, concealed lighting and central heating [hardly 'central' or even 'heating' by later standards!] and will seat rather more people than Pembroke Hall – considerably more if the balcony overhead be used....

We hope the foregoing gives no wrong impression of grandiloquence or lavishness. All is simple, yet with a simplicity akin to graciousness that will become beauty when the chapel is furnished and endowed with spiritual power.

When furnished! Alas, the furnishings from the Hall are dusty, shabby, scarred, the curtains and carpets deeply impregnated – as is everything else – with a pulverised mortar dust, adhesive almost beyond belief. A formidable task opens. No mere dusting or banging will suffice, but a wholehearted scrubbing, perhaps in many waters, will be called for. So far as possible we shall retain and repair our furnishings, partly for association's sake, partly because battle scars are honourable. But our organ lies in matchwood back in the shambles which was Pembroke Hall, with many another article smashed beyond redemption.... But think of the thrill of making ready, of reconstruction!

ANGELUS, *January 1941*

Two of the willing team who put their backs into this 'formidable task' (our editor did not exaggerate) were the Brameld twins, Mary and Elizabeth. They were only children then, still at school; but with their mother (Sister 'Hope', later to become a pillar of service in the Lodge), they scrubbed and cleaned and polished with a will.

We mention them particularly because a few years later Mary was called by White Eagle to fill the place at the organ left empty (except for a few more temporary helpers) when 'Brother John' died early in 1945. This she continued to do through the 1950s and 1960s, and indeed still regularly takes her place at the organ of the London Lodge, though it is a much more sophisticated instrument now than the small Positive organ (shown in the photograph on page 53) – one manual, four stops and no pedals, but dear to our hearts – which replaced the one destroyed in Pembroke Hall.

And so, after much hard but happy work, the new home for White Eagle's work was opened and dedicated by him on Saturday, 22 March, at three o'clock, and thus began a whole new era in the story of the White Eagle Lodge.

In the course of his talk at the dedication White Eagle said: 'I tell you that if this temple be cast down tomorrow, it will be rebuilt

A glimpse of the main chapel at St Mary Abbots Place shortly after the opening. Compare the later pictures, on pp. 53, 114 and 126

Opposite page: the entrance to 9 St Mary Abbots Place, probably just after the War

THE STORY OF THE WHITE EAGLE LODGE

again, and rebuilt again and yet again; for this is the law of the Cosmos, making for resurrection and life eternal'.

Thanks be to God, we were not called upon to put White Eagle's words to the test – although we did almost immediately have three fire-bombs descend on the roof of the Lodge. They miraculously burnt themselves out. Another fell in 1943, when an unknown hero rushed in from the street and volunteered to go up into the roof, where he put out the fire blazing there. He then disappeared as anonymously as he had come.

Quietly and steadily, and in spite of the difficulties, dangers and restrictions of wartime, the work grew and developed both on the outer plane and in inner strength. It was a period of rebuilding and consolidation. In ANGELUS of October 1941 the six Principles of the Lodge, formulated under White Eagle's guidance, were printed for the first time, together with an interpretation of the Lodge symbol of the Cross of Light within the Circle of Light with the Star at its centre. The formulation of these principles seemed to establish the independent being of the Lodge and, looking back, they strengthened the work at the inner level – perhaps they would be better described as giving us a foundation on which to work.

1943 was a specially notable year. In April the Lodge was approved for the solemnisation of marriages, and in November the first entry was made in our registers – Joan's marriage to John Hodgson. (We little knew then what a cornerstone of the Lodge John, who was still serving in the R.A.F. at the time, was to become – but no doubt White Eagle did!). Two years later, as the War ended, they had their first child, christened Rose Mary (Rosemary, now now Rose Elliot).

We were now beginning to find that our premises at No. 9 were hardly big enough to contain the expanding work, and therefore were thankful when in the autumn the owners, who also possessed the adjoining house, No. 9a, agreed to allow us to include the latter in our agreement at a rental we could just manage. We were able, by making a door between the two buildings, to add another large sanctuary, the present Brotherhood Chapel, which, once the threat of bombings was past, became the permanent place for the inner teachings, the meditation groups and of course the Brotherhood itself. 9a also gave us living accommodation that released room in the main Lodge for a row of little healing chapels, quieter than the old ones, which had been situated on the balcony, where healers and patients were often disturbed by noise and conversation.

The new chapels were dedicated in the autumn at a service attended by fifty people, chiefly Lodge healers. White Eagle said, in his dedication: 'Let nothing be too much trouble when you are dealing with the heart and soul of your brother man. Be tender, considerate and patient – for we are all children of God, who is patient and tender with us all....' We called the healing chapels the

Joan with daugher Rosemary, born in June 1945 and now Mrs Rose Elliot

THE STORY OF THE WHITE EAGLE LODGE

Mary Chapel, the Joseph, the Sara Burdett and the Christopher; and they were partitions of the room, outside the new Brotherhood chapel, which now comprises simply the Minesta chapel. At the far end was a Grace Chapel for private prayer and meditation.

'Why the Sara Burdett Chapel?', some readers may ask.

'Sara' Burdett, whose Brotherhood name inspired Jenny Dent in calling her daughter Sara

Some years ago, before the White Eagle Lodge came into being, and when White Eagle was speaking at various centres and churches in London, one of his most faithful adherents was a certain lady dignified of presence, with a clear, bright colour, and beautiful silver hair. Once White Eagle asked her if she had ever been associated with Annie Besant.* She replied in the affirmative. After this incident we came to know her a little better, and discovered that she had been a personal friend and secretary of 'A.B.' …. The passing of 'A.B.' had brought this phase of our new friend's activities to a close.

When the opening of the White Eagle Lodge was planned, and when premises were found, one of the first to offer her services was Miss Burdett – 'Sara', as she became generally and affectionately known in the Lodge…. Those who worshipped in Pembroke Hall … will recall a figure, tall and upright, and white of hair, seated in the front row of chairs with a note-book and pencil, intent and businesslike.

Ivan Cooke, in ANGELUS, *June 1942*

As well as 'taking down' White Eagle's messages, Sara (christened Susan) had brought qualities to the work that were truly manifold: ability in administration, all the experience of her association with the leaders of the Theosophical Society, and wise advice and unfailing support. She worked hard getting the organisation of the healing onto a sound footing and she was a first-rate healer herself. She had died in 1941, broken as much by the War as by age.

A Thanksgiving Service had been held for her in the Lodge; and for John Hodgson it had been one of the earliest meetings there he attended. He writes, 'It was my first experience of a thanksgiving service, as opposed to the orthodox, sad memorial services which I had attended in my youth. I was struck by the dignity of the presentation, lack of gloom, with the thanksgiving for a life of faithful service the keynote throughout. Most impressive, it was a big step forward on my journey'.

To return to 1943. That year Alison Innes, who was later to give so many people their first welcome as they entered the Lodge, first

*Annie Besant, social reformer, sometime socialist, President of the Theosophical Society, Co-Freemason, friend of George Bernard Shaw, Jiddu Krishnamurti, and Gandhi; writer and mystic, born 1847. She was deeply admired by Minesta; her death in 1933 indeed would have freed Sara Burdett to begin full involvement with the White Eagle Lodge.

came to work here, originally part-time, to help Joan with the healing and astrological work (the latter just developing in the Lodge), and then two years later as a full-time worker in the Lodge team, which she continued to be more or less until her passing in 1987. Today's 'Pearl' Chapel in the London Lodge is given the name White Eagle gave her, in recognition of all she brought to the work.

Alison Innes

In the mean time, things had not been entirely quiet on the publishing front. In November 1943 came the first *White Eagle Calendar*. It is intriguing to read in ANGELUS, 'Permission from the Ministry of Supply had to be obtained before our Calendar could be printed, a protracted process'!

In addition, between June 1942 and October 1944 all four volumes of the first series of SPIRITUAL UNFOLDMENT books were published, roughly a book every six months. Also published during the period was Joan's WISDOM IN THE STARS and what was then called PRAYERS OF THE NEW AGE (a title today remembered in PRAYER, MINDFULNESS AND INNER CHANGE – a much-expanded successor).

Despite the expansion of the Lodge work implied in our memories of these years, they were difficult times – as anyone who lived through them will remember. There were the black-out, the air-raids and the flying bombs; the food shortages and restrictions of all kinds; the ever-present scenes of destruction, the depressing newspaper headlines. It is amazing to us that not only was Minesta able to continue her spiritual work in these conditions, but that some very wonderful and sustaining teaching was given during those years of strain and stress. During the worst periods of danger and through the winter months all services were held during daylight hours. In 1944 the Lodge actually closed for an extended summer break, because the danger of flying glass from its roofs was too great. We remember one Inner Teaching given in what is now an interview room for healing patients (but a larger room then than today, having been two major sets of alterations)* when, as we sat listening to White Eagle's loving words, there was a large thud close by and the earth shook as a V-2 bomb landed not far away. White Eagle remained unmoved and we all felt safe and enfolded in angels' wings.

Another of the publications in 1943 was a second edition, with a fine cover design, of THE CHRISTIAN MYSTERIES. *Much of the teaching in this is now incorporated into* THE LIGHT BRINGER

Ylana writes, 'There was another occasion when Joan and I, having sought shelter under our office desk during one of the worst night raids, were inexpressibly comforted by the awareness (which came to each of us independently) of being sheltered by great white wings, and we knew that White Eagle was with us and all was well'. These were the sort of experiences which sustained White Eagle's wider family too, along with the unceasing reassurance of his teach-

---

*The original room disappeared around 1960 and became part vestibule to the Main Chapel and part side-chapel, a room known as the Grace Chapel until the refurbishments of 1995, when out of it was created what we now call 'Peace's Room'.

ing. Here, for instance, is a benediction from a wartime service:

And now, peace be in your hearts ... peace ... and know that our love shines as the Sun, giving you all that you need, day by day. That is it! ... one day at a time ... day by day. God is in His Heaven; all is well!

ANGELUS, *February 1942*

The level of spiritual work done by the Brotherhood during this time, proposed and promised by Brother Faithful in THE WHITE BROTHERHOOD at the outset of war, is not to be underestimated. In the 1990s it was the subject of a Channel Four documentary on British TV, later published in book form, which included a substantial interview with Ylana. She described the regular projections of light to unknown locations, indicated by White Eagle but unknown to his earthly brethren, all round the world, and how the locations would then be in news reports.

When V.E. Day came at last, on 8 May 1945, it was celebrated by the happiest of impromptu parties; blackout was torn down, the sandbags were removed from the courtyard, and we all turned our faces hopefully to the sun. Later, the war ended in the Far East in the way White Eagle had described in his talk on 10 September 1939. Despite the crises of 1939 and 1940, the Lodge had come through the war, and had come through it having found an identity, and with the discovery of the value of working together. It had gained, out of an apparent disaster, premises placed right beside one of London's main streets, but where visitors can almost forget they are in London – where the loudest sound is often the birdsong from the neighbouring gardens. Despite the danger from air-raids and the inconvenience of the blackout the Brotherhood's work had continued almost without a break, with brothers attending unfailingly throughout the War; and by some miraculous act of preservation no-one engaged on their Lodge business ever came to harm through enemy action (as, indeed, White Eagle had foretold).

This does not of course mean that White Eagle brethren somehow managed to opt out of armed service. Quite to the contrary: John Hodgson served in the Desert Campaigns, for instance, and we can see the uniform on the member in the picture, Bill Patterson. Bill was an artist and his drawings are to be found adorning ANGELUS and the some of the wartime books. He was one of a whole circle whose introduction to the Lodge is linked with Teddy Dent (whom we met on p. 22): they include Nancie, who became Bill's wife; Betty Barber, Teddy's half-sister, and Gerry Clarke, who with his wife Anne later ran a White Eagle group in Lymington, Hampshire. And, of course, Teddy's wife Madge and son Geoffrey.

Throughout the War, all those members engaged on active service were held in the protection of the cross of Light within the circle

Bill Patterson holding his daughter Anne, who today works at St John's Retreat Center in Texas

of Light by groups specially formed for this purpose, and many of those on active service subsequently had remarkable stories to tell of how they were helped, protected and guided. One of these was related to the Brotherhood in May 1940 by the officer himself. After the collapse of the French armies his brigade was surrounded by the enemy and likely to be annihilated. He drew upon the protective power of the Light, which he knew was being given to him by those in the unseen. Miraculously, the brigade was guided out of danger and escaped at Dunkirk. The brigadier was our Brother 'Peter', James Hamilton, who was to bring spiritual strength and the power of example to the Lodge for many more years.

The Brotherhood work throughout the war was under very clear and direct guidance from White Eagle – and we do believe, humbly, that the Brotherhood made a very real contribution to the victory of the forces of Light during the 'years of fire': the work for which the Brotherhood had been called together in the early 1930s. In moments of great crisis on the battlefield, or in the air or at sea, White Eagle told us, many through their sacrifice or their fulfilment of duty touch the spiritual forces and receive illumination. They make 'contact with this supreme Light; and you can help them on the inner or spiritual planes, perhaps more effectively than can thousands on the material plane' (THE BROTHERHOOD TEACHING).

The Lodge had survived the War and it had also grown, in numbers and in reputation. The first 'Daughter Lodge' (Edinburgh) was followed in 1942 by a second one, also in Scotland, in Glasgow. The membership of the whole Lodge had grown, too, from the initial hundred and twenty to about three hundred at the end of the War. Moreover the brothers and closer members of the Lodge had worked together through great trials for up to ten years (in a few cases longer). Even those who lived many miles from the Lodge were linked to the centre by ANGELUS, which had proved a spiritual lifeline to so many during the war years. This was particularly true of the period between the destruction of the first Lodge and the opening of the new premises, when it was our one link (on the outer plane) with our friends and members. One of our friends described to us for the first edition of this book how eagerly she awaited the magazine each month, throughout the War. The regular messages from White Eagle in ANGELUS were much looked forward to (particularly as there were fewer White Eagle books available), interspersed as they were with good-humoured and down-to-earth wisdom from the magazine's editor, Ivan Cooke. Now the Lodge entered a new period, found a new focus to which the effort of the members and brothers could be turned after the very concentrated work which the War had demanded.

Sister Radiant (Kathleen Fleming) one of the Glasgow Lodge pioneers, initiated in 1937

CHAPTER III

New Lands

Minesta in the woods near Headley Down, dressed in Native American costume

Rake Village

ON 24 FEBRUARY 1936, two days after the opening of the Lodge, and doubtless awakening tender memories of Burstow, White Eagle had said: 'We wish you to hold in the invisible the vision of that home in the country, which some day will come into being in spite of all the difficulties and obstacles. Be patient. Never doubt, but hold the vision of this centre, this home in the country.... It will be the inner mystical centre'. Eight years later, on New Year's Eve, 1944, speaking privately to the family at their little cottage at Headley Down, Hampshire, he left them in no doubt that the time had come to look for this home, to which he had referred at intervals throughout the years since leaving Burstow. He said, 'The place will be found by the Brotherhood invisible ... it will lie between here and the ancient city of Winchester, it will lie on high ground, and it will be sheltered and screened from cold winds by a belt of trees. It will look out to the view of the setting sun, and on the other side a view of the rising sun. There will be pasture land and orchard; a sweet herb garden and a rose garden. Flowers and flowering shrubs will be there and it will be a place where the Brotherhood of old have tilled the soil.... It is a fair place with a fair name. In the course of 1945, you will be guided to find it'.

After giving some further detailed description of the property White Eagle added: 'A community of service will be established there.... Brothers will come to it for quiet and refreshment and training; but the primary purpose is ... to establish a centre of power, a centre from which will ray forth, not only in your day, but for long, long time after this incarnation has passed, rays of light and power which will eventually bring the whole of Britain under its influence. It is a work with a small beginning, but a vast future.' (1966 Newsletter.)

And so it was that we began looking for the property in the final months of the war. In the second half of April 1945, returning from inspecting a property in the centre of Hampshire, an unplanned diversion was made to another house that was on the market – at Rake, a village near Petersfield in the same county. The aspect and the setting, the name of the house and the locality, fitted what White Eagle had said exactly.

We shall always remember that first sight of New Lands, standing warm and friendly on the hilltop, in the evening sun. We did not have an order to view but were allowed to walk round the garden. It was a mass of wild daffodils.

And so, against all the advice of the experts and with the help of two very good friends, New Lands was purchased and the work there began to develop according to White Eagle's directions. The timing of his guidance on this, as on so many other matters, was exact, since even while negotiations were in progress for the purchase of the property, house prices began the upward spiral that has continued ever since.

New Lands was dedicated by White Eagle on 29 September (the Feast of St Michael and All Angels):

Some forty of the brethren and members of the Lodge attended the service. The month of September granted its one perfect day's weather on that Saturday, and nothing marred any moment of it. Since then the spirit and the power are gathering within the chapel at New Lands. May it be that in the months and years to

The aerial photo of New Lands above was taken in or before 1956. Note the beauty of the setting and the flower beds all round the house. The two greenhouses were later removed as the structures became unsafe, and were to form the site for the office extension in the 1980s; water tanks below then became a cellar!

come the light will reach, help and bless many other lives. In his dedication White Eagle said, 'Beloved brethren, we in the spirit realm rejoice with you on this day of sunshine and power.… This building is a home of peace and harmony and light. It has been prepared not for a few years but for centuries. Brethren of a very ancient Order have dwelt here before.… We hope that in this house simplicity, harmony and brotherly love will ever be preserved. May all work together as a team … may the best always arise in the heart; and may God manifest through the brooms and the saucepans and the dusters of the home; may Christ manifest at the table, in the garden, in the flowers.… Thus may there be established here a community of service, a Brotherhood of the ancient order of the Great White Light.

ANGELUS, November 1945

Those who know New Lands today, who come in their cars past the Temple and sweep round the next bend into New Lands drive; who make, perhaps, for the office door, behind which they know are offices on three floors, housing a staff of twenty or more, will find it difficult to picture the New Lands of the late 1940s: unless, perhaps, they make for New Lands front door itself, or walk out into the garden; where, we hope, they can be sure that the monastic peace of New Lands is preserved. The photograph opposite shows the differences. In those days there was only the one gateway from the road, the one into the gravelled drive at the top of the hill, through the oak gates hung on stone posts that are still there. This passed the back door (screened by trees and shrubs, as were the adjacent potting shed and greenhouses) before opening into the front drive. No road continued beyond as it does now: a high, thick conifer hedge which separated Garden Cottage from New Lands stretched right along the drive until it gave way to a little walk past the front lawn, beside an azalea bed.

The original altar at New Lands chapel, on the north wall, set up for a christening (c. 1952)

The first retreat at New Lands was held in the week it opened, September 1945: but it was, at first, a summer centre; and a satellite, too, of the London Lodge. A thrilling and yet an exhausting task it was, getting the house together for the opening day, and an added workload for Minesta, having a country house to run while her London commitments remained. There were twelve retreats in each of the first two or three summers, so we see her finishing a busy week in London and setting off for New Lands to prepare for a retreat that began on the Monday. She took a full part in the running of the house at first, even down to the ironing. As the farewells ceased at the end of the week, it was London again to think about, and a week that might include the monthly inner teaching or a White Eagle address on the Sunday. Ylana, as General Secretary of the Lodge, divided her time between London and New

Lands (with Alison Innes, 'Pearl', often holding the fort in London in the meanwhile), and normally cooked for the Retreats. Joan was not so free to help, with a small child to look after; but when John was 'demobbed' at the end of the War he turned down a very good job in the world, and threw himself wholeheartedly into the White Eagle work at a time when help was urgently needed. He was appointed Treasurer and was thus able to take over from Ylana part of the burden of her work. John remembers how White Eagle said to him when he came into the work, 'If you are going to work for White Eagle you have to be prepared to do anything'. He was, and he did!

John's task as Treasurer was no easy one. The cost of New Lands dwarfed the Lodge's resources, and the late 1940s and 1950s were a time of great stringency, nursing a mortgage and several loans – in which the Lodge lived, even at the best of times, from hand to mouth – so John was constantly having to pay money from one Lodge account to another so that bills could be met. Often they were only met by a seeming miracle: an unexpected donation or a small legacy (this remains true today, although thankfully it now applies more to the extraordinary bills than the ordinary ones). The publications were in particular difficulty: little or no profit was made from sales, so there was no cash in hand for the publication of a new title, and one solution successfully tried in 1957 was the subscription scheme launched for the MORNING LIGHT series. But the greatest burden required more than the Treasurer's agility, and in a sense it also gave the greatest opportunity, for it brought the members together in a common effort.

This came in 1946. Hardly had we taken breath from the purchase of New Lands (and with its mortgage outstanding) than we were faced with the expiration of the lease on St Mary Abbots Place. However the owner, Mrs Calderon, who wished to sell, gave Minesta first refusal of an offer for the whole property (the two houses, 9 and 9a) for £15,000. We made a gesture of looking at other properties, but the guidance from the spirit was clear – that 9 St Mary Abbots Place was the Lodge home. So there was really no choice but to go forward in faith, as always; the offer was accepted, and a Building Fund launched; and in ANGELUS Minesta wrote:

I am happy to tell you that arrangements are in progress for the purchase of the present Lodge premises. The sum of £15,000 will be needed before we can have the building entirely free, as White Eagle has said it will be in due course, and of this sum we have to raise £6,000 before the end of May 1947. This will require every effort we can make.

ANGELUS, November 1946

The last statement was an understatement, we think! In February 1947 we read: 'The day of completion of the purchase of the White Eagle Lodge building is May 7th next, so we have three months to go and £3,000 to raise. It is going to be a big task. We shall carry it through together'. And we did! The purchase was duly completed. But it was ten years and more of hard work, in which every one played their own part, before the mortgage, and the interest-free loans that had been so important to us in 1947, could be paid off. The financial struggle of 1947 had a far-reaching consequence beyond the London Lodge, for it hastened the Lodge's becoming a registered charity, so that donations could be protected by guarantees about their use, and tax could be claimed back. It also produced the prototype of what became a tradition for the rest of the twentieth century, namely our annual Christmas Fairs: a bring-and-buy sale held on 23 November 1946, which was followed by a spring bazaar at a hall in Hammersmith in April 1947.

In 1948 came the first of a series of Trust Deeds by which – by 1953 – not only both the Lodge properties but also all the publications of the Lodge (the copyright of White Eagle's teachings), were transferred from private to public ownership to be held in Trust in perpetuity for the purposes laid down in the Deeds. This major step was not taken without much heart-searching by Minesta, as can be imagined, but it did mean that the Lodge could go forward guarded and guided by the ideals and principles first given to us by White Eagle. They placed the whole work on a secure foundation both materially and spiritually.

For this and very much more, we have to thank a true friend, referred to earlier, Noel Gabriel. His own spiritual insight coupled with a deep devotion to White Eagle and to White Eagle's medium, and later his knowledge of the law, were the gifts he brought to the work. Such gifts enabled him to formulate these various Trusts and to pilot them through the maze of legal formalities. He served White Eagle devotedly since he first came to us as a young man, and it is hardly surprising therefore to read of White Eagle saying to him, during a group at the Lodge in 1938; 'Remember, my brother who studies the law, that you are preparing yourself as a channel for the White Brotherhood. You will be used in the service of the Brotherhood'.

Looking back down the years, one of the remarkable things that stands out about the story of the Lodge is that always, when specialised knowledge and help has been needed, the right person has been there to give that help, and with it their heart. It is as though long before we all came into incarnation the plans were laid and each one detailed for his task.

But let us return to 1947, a very important year for the Lodge work in America. ANGELUS spoke of a Mrs Olive Robinson who

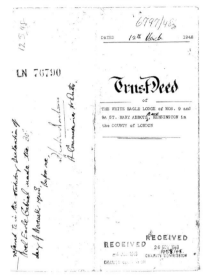

The 1948 Trust Deed

Olive Robinson

on a short visit to England last year, attended a service at the London Lodge and from that moment was inspired to carry White Eagle's teaching to the States and to found a Lodge in New Jersey. The result is a veritable proof of unwavering faith, courage and selfless service on her part and that of her husband who, guided … from the inner planes … brought into being the beautiful little temple now dedicated to the work an understatement, we think…. The building … was constructed single-handed by Mr Robinson – even to the cutting of the timber and making the concrete blocks of which the walls are built, the installing of electric light and the plumbing. Working steadily from 4 a.m. each day throughout the intense heat of the summer the building gradually took shape and was completed by the opening date, August 17th 1947.

ANGELUS, November 1947

Looking back from the altar in the little New Jersey chapel

Alas – this, the first overseas Daughter Lodge of the Brotherhood, is no longer in being, for John Robinson passed over two or three years after its founding and although Olive continued with love and zeal for many years eventually the time came when age forced her to retire too. Nevertheless the seeds sown some sixty years ago have borne rich fruit in the form of the Temple and supporting groups all over the United States. It was at Olive's request that Brother Faithful produced the first Correspondence Course in Spiritual Unfoldment which she ran with happy effect for many years.

In 1948, the first children's service was held in the Lodge, the beginning of the work with children that Joan began and which is now such a valuable and important aspect of the White Eagle work. Another 'first' for 1948 was the formation of a group specially for the absent healing of animals; and some time later it is rather nice to read in ANGELUS of some of the cases.

Pride of place had better be given to a Sealyham dog aged fourteen and a half years, suffering, regrettably, from bad temper, having bitten various people – from which it may be argued that his teeth remain in good order. Since treatment by the group his temper has greatly improved.

Another patient was a parrot, suffering from sickness and moulting, which has recovered. Love and protection was also given to a young elephant over a period of several months when it was known that it was being cruelly treated while being trained. Results are not known in this case. Another loved dog was treated for shock after being knocked about by a gang of hooligans. He has now recovered, A huge Pyrenean dog suffering from eczema was also successfully treated.

ANGELUS, October 1950

Joan, around 1948

THE STORY OF THE WHITE EAGLE LODGE

A White Eagle wedding in Edinburgh: Mary and Alan Hershey, February 1952

In September 1949 came the first Chain of Fellowship article, a feature of ANGELUS and later of STELLA POLARIS, which continued for fifty-seven years through to 2006, when Jenny preferred to call it 'Links of Light'. It was both a personal letter and an introduction to readers' letters. In that first one Minesta wrote:

> I hope to form a Chain with our ever-increasing family through-out the world as its link.... Brief extracts will be given from the letters received, particularly from our readers overseas, so that there will follow a building-up of this family spirit throughout the world like that which we have endeavoured to establish at the London Lodge and the New Lands home. By this means, I hope all our readers will feel they are in personal touch and can share each others' interests.
>
> *ANGELUS, September 1949*

Letters quoted came from Iceland, Australia, New Jersey and South Africa, so it will be seen how far White Eagle's teaching had already spread. The first of the much-loved 'Gentle Brother' series appeared in STELLA POLARIS in 1953 and still continues.

A final memory of 1949 is the making of the first White Eagle gramophone record. It was a ten-inch disc, running at 78 r.p.m., and it played for seven minutes. To the best of our memory it was made at the suggestion of a friend who had the recording equipment, which he brought to the Lodge with him. Recording was a very different and more taxing matter in those days. The speaker had to record it just right, or forever hold his peace; and to the exact length. We remember White Eagle's patience and love as he repeated his message for the record two or three times in order to make the break at the appropriate moment. What amazed us was that although it was apparently spontaneous, each time he recorded it the words were to all intents and purposes the same. This certainty about his words was a very clear proof, if we needed one, that White Eagle was entirely separate from and superior to his medium.

Frank and Bee Wharhirst

When New Lands opened there was, of course, no local congregation, and no Lodge community there other than retreat participants and whichever members of Minesta's family happened to be there. Slowly, however, not only did the immediate family grow, but the wider family as well. Outside retreat weeks, the early Brotherhood ceremonies were never more than six strong, but these few brothers kept to their service faithfully through the 1950s. Among them were Frank and Beatrice Wharhirst, 'Frank' and 'Brown Lady', Minesta's brother-in-law and sister, who for the first few years lived actually on the estate at New Lands. A healing group was also held, chiefly with these same brothers. After the early years, the New Lands work grew faster, for under White

Eagle's direction we began to hold activities in the winter months as well as during the summer. His instruction was that we should 'keep New Lands warm, on all planes' – and indeed a little community was growing round New Lands, wanting regular services and groups. Thus a monthly Worship and Communion was started, and children's services and meditation groups.

Joan and John's second daughter Joan Minesta, now Jenny Dent, was born after the terrible winter of 1946–7. New Lands was beginning to be a place for children to grow up. The year was also marked by Brother Faithful's hospitalisation for a short period – something which had a good side to it, for it was in convalescence that he took up painting as a hobby and therapy. To this day, his much-loved paintings adorn New Lands and the London Lodge.

Family Hodgson:
Jenny, John,
Rosemary, Joan

In 1950 a new strength was brought into the work when Geoffrey Hayward joined the family. It was Geoffrey's support and clear understanding of White Eagle's vision of 'the home in the country' that had helped to give Minesta the courage to make that vision a reality. Coming from outside, he had an appreciation of the profundity and scope of White Eagle's teaching, and of the future of the work, which we who had our heads more buried in the business of every day probably lacked. On his marriage to Ylana in 1951 he ceased his work as education officer in the R.A.F. and, like John before him, gave himself wholly to serving White Eagle and the Brotherhood. His coming was to have a profound effect on the work at many levels, but very particularly upon the books and publications, which were to become his special responsibility.

An event not entirely unconnected with his coming was the transformation of ANGELUS into the magazine so well-known today, STELLA POLARIS, in December 1951. With the growing volume of work and increasing difficulties in the printing trade, it was becoming harder and harder to produce a monthly magazine. The cost of production was rising all the time, leading to an unacceptable subscription rate. We were being guided, too, to reach out to a greater public by including articles on a wider range of subjects (but with White Eagle's teaching always as the foundation). So STELLA POLARIS was born, with an entirely new format and clear typeface, to appear every two months; since when it has gone from strength to strength.

But we must go back to ANGELUS for a moment, for it was in February 1951 that the words of our Prayer for Humanity were made public and printed there. Probably this was the first time that all the White Eagle family had joined together in prayer to send out the Light, using the same words. Later came the 'call to prayer' at the magical hours, and the dedication to the service of the Light that has become so basic to the work.

In the same issue we read of Joan's election to the Board of the

THE STORY OF THE WHITE EAGLE LODGE

*Family Hayward:
Geoffrey and Ylana, with
Jeremy and Colum*

Faculty of Astrological Studies and of her earning the Faculty's Diploma – an indication of the important place of the study of the spiritual aspects and significance of the science of Astrology to the White Eagle work as a whole.

On 12th March we had a specially beautiful ceremony at the [London] Lodge, the first of its kind ever held. This was the ordination of two … Ministers who have served a long period of probation and training for their new office … Mrs Joan Hodgson (Joan Cooke) and Mrs Geoffrey Hayward (Ylana Cooke). Their ordination and dedication of their lives to the work of The White Eagle Lodge is particularly significant because they are also ordained as the future Trustees of the work of the White Eagle Lodge.

[And, in the same year:]

John Hodgson, having served the required period of training and unfoldment, was ordained by White Eagle as a Minister of the White Eagle Lodge on July 2nd last. May a blessing rest upon his calling and his ministry.

ANGELUS, April and September 1951

With the steady increase of the activities at New Lands, the focus of the whole work began to change, and in 1953 all the administrative side of the work was moved down to the country. The volume of office work, both on the healing side (Joan) and for the General Secretary (Ylana – now with twins, Colum and Jeremy, born in February 1952, to look after!) was such that it could no longer be done in a general reception office, which was all the space that London afforded. The move certainly made the work much easier – particularly the despatch and storage of books, the volume of which was increasing all the time. We do wonder what we should have felt if we could have foreseen the office buildings of today!

In 1954 the first Garden Party at New Lands was held. It rained solidly and continually from early morning until the last guests departed. But somehow we managed to enjoy ourselves jamming every room and every passage of the house. Annette Mills (of 'Muffin the Mule' fame) opened the Garden Party, nothing daunted. Her charm saved the day. We have since learnt to work on the weather and to seek the co-operation of the angels and the spirits of the sun, mostly with success!

Looking back, one thinks of the 1950s as difficult years – years of struggle to make ends meet, with the heavy burden of mortgage repayments overshadowing everything. As well as the running expenses, there was also the responsibility of the spiritual wellbeing of the whole work, both in London and at New Lands, which still fell largely upon Minesta, with Brother Faithful always beside

EARLY YEARS AT NEW LANDS : A CELEBRATION

From the start, New Lands activities centred on the week-long retreats to which members were invited to participate. On this page, the top pair date from as early as 1949. The middle pair are just slightly later. Bottom left is 1956, while bottom right is not precisely known; maybe just a little later. See also p. 157.

The top pair of pictures show garden features many years ago: the 'toadstool' at the foot of a tree in a corner of the garden that now is road; and Monks' Walk before the Temple drive was built. The awning over the Chapel window in the picture on the left shows that this view was taken before the altar was transferred from the side of the room to its present position.

Below, the 1956 Garden Party was opened by Joan because of Minesta's indisposition; while probably the same year, Ylana leads camp fire singing at the end, with a choir behind her.

her. The new ministers took their share, but were still very much in training, and their involvement was more with the secretarial and administrative than the spiritual side. That in itself was none too easy, with young families. Although she was for a while quite seriously ill in 1956, we do not think Minesta's courage ever really failed her, and always White Eagle was strong and hopeful and forward-looking, bolstering our faith whenever it wavered; helping us all the time to understand spiritual law and to live with our vision on the Star. They were valuable, strengthening years, and prepared us for the further expansion of the 1960s.

Minesta's 'Chain of Fellowship' in April 1955 contained another fundraising challenge to her members!

In two years' time (that is, February 1957) the White Eagle Lodge will have carried on this work for twenty-one years.... I think [this] calls for a special Anniversary celebration, and to mark this event it has been proposed to collect a Million Pennies as a Twenty-First Birthday Present to White Eagle's work.... If all our 4000 friends would give 3d. a week for two years the Lodge will be freed of the heavy debt and funds will be freed to spread White Eagle's teaching....

When we came to New Lands, the beeches along the bank over the Monks' Walk were still young, and inspired a painting Brother Faithful recopied many times. The pond, as the picture shows, was protected by high heather.

THE STORY OF THE WHITE EAGLE LODGE

In the entrance of the Lodge in London there stands the model of a Lighthouse, with a large collecting box. It will be lit from within, and as the number of pennies increases so the light will grow duly brighter.

We hope that this light will be the sign and symbol of the progress of the work of the White Eagle Lodge, both spiritually and materially.

3d, the old 'threepenny bit', was not very much; we guess it felt a little bit like a 20p coin does today. Two years later the million-pennies target was achieved; and a few months later, in time for our twenty-second anniversary, the London Lodge was finally cleared of all outstanding debt. Minesta promptly launched a second million-penny fund, to help with the running expenses! She had a great belief in involving everyone in whatever project was on hand; in drawing us all together to meet a challenge so that everyone felt – and was – part of every venture. It was her inspiration that built up the wonderful family spirit that has grown and grown and remains the strength of the work.

In 1955 we produced the first of our annual Newsletters for Members. It took the form of a retrospective view of the previous year and appeared in duplicated form on three foolscap (8 x 13 inch) pages, close-typed. It was very much appreciated by Members everywhere, helping again to draw all together into a closer family; and also was specially appreciated by the growing number of overseas Members, for whom it brought the Lodge and its various activities close. An interesting point was made in this Newsletter:

> The character of the Sunday services has become more devotional by the substitution for the most part of a period of spiritual communion, for the usual clairvoyance. It is possible that this means that fewer of the general public are attracted to the Service, but we feel regular worshippers generally prefer the new form.
>
> *Retrospect 1954 (sent out 1955)*

Indeed they did, and the London Lodge congregations grew.

1955 saw two major publications, the first to appear under the imprint of the newly-created White Eagle Publishing Trust (1953). They were HEALING (now HEALING BY THE SPIRIT), the printing of which was subsidised by two friends in the U.S.A.; and MEDITATION, which probably more than any other book to date set a standard and a guide to the White Eagle way of life, and sold more widely too. It broke new ground. Joan later explained the story behind it.

> It was during [the] war years that for a short time Minesta had the opportunity to study meditation according to Eastern methods.

Main Chapel of the London Lodge at around this time; note the edge of the Positive organ to the right, referred to elsewhere. Below, Minesta at Lordat in Ariége, France, on her return visit there in 1957 (see over, p. 54)

The teacher, obviously brought to her by White Eagle, helped her to see even more clearly the difference between what one might perhaps call spontaneous psychic gifts, and the conscious unfoldment of spiritual awareness through aspiration, and the mental discipline of meditation. For many years, White Eagle had been gradually bringing us to this point in his spiritual unfoldment groups, but contact with this teacher brought about an expansion of consciousness which enabled White Eagle to take us even further, henceforward the training was to become deeper and more along the lines described in Minesta's book MEDITATION.

Joan Hodgson, 'Personal Recollections of Minesta and White Eagle', STELLA POLARIS, August-September 1980

Today it would be most intriguing to know who the eastern teacher was who brought such a gift. Henceforth, married to the strong visualisation form of meditation derived from development and unfoldment training, there was a new emphasis on the silence, the breath and a chosen mantram. The book exceptionally included teaching from the records of an inner group that White Eagle had been addressing since its foundation at Easter 1946. The Rose Group was attended by Noel Gabriel, 'Radiance', and Paul Beard, as well as Minesta and her immediate family.

Retrospect 1956 makes the first mention of the group of young people drawn together as a working band, led by the enthusiasm and devotion of Michael Collishaw – together with Diana Higgins and Edna Taylor, and later Heather Taylor, her sister, and Geoffrey Dent – all of these now (to our great loss) in the land of Light. They christened themselves – or was it White Eagle who christened them? – 'the Eaglets'; and many were their good works and their happy times together. Year after year they would come down to 'spring clean' New Lands and do various redecoration jobs; and in the London Lodge they mounted plays and entertainments for the enjoyment of members and the benefit of the funds. They would hold regular monthly discussions as well as enjoying many social occasions together; and at all the major Lodge functions the Eaglets were in evidence behind the scenes lending a hand.

And so we come to 1957, the coming-of-age of the Lodge. In the previous year, in order to assist her convalescence, Paul and Rosemary Beard had taken Minesta and Faithful on holiday to France. While there they spent some time at Lordat, where the two of them had worked with the Polaires twenty-five years previously. It was a very happy and powerful renewing of the old link and a touching again of the magic of the Polaire Star – almost, it seemed, a gift from the Brotherhood, of renewed strength and power for the coming-of-age.

Of the many announcements made in that year, perhaps the most significant was that about the creation of the Outer Brotherhood.

Opposite page: the Twenty-first Birthday Service in London and the Members' Party that followed it

Michael Collishaw around 1950; Edna Taylor as a 'land girl' in the War. Her sister Heather is the person serving in the lower photo opposite

It is White Eagle's wish that an 'Outer Brotherhood' of the White Eagle Lodge be instituted in the New Year, under the symbol of the Star.... If you have been a member for a year or longer [we now ask two years minimum] and are in sympathy with the ideal of an organised spiritual Brotherhood ... will you write to me? You will then receive full particulars of this plan of the Wise Ones to form an outer membership of our Inner Brotherhood.

Grace Cooke, in STELLA POLARIS, *December 1956–January 1957*

More and more, as the years passed, people were coming into the Lodge because of the opportunity for service it offered. Uneasy world conditions, together with a growing spiritual awareness, stim-

CONTENTS

I GLEAM OF DAWN 7
Truth lies within Yourself - Man's Great Descent

II THE MIRACLE OF LIGHT 16
Life is governed by Law - On Miracles

III THE QUICKENING SUN 26
Worship of the Light - The Christ Radiance The Secret of Perfect Health

IV THE LIGHT THAT IS LIFE 35
The Elder Brethren - The World Teacher The Saving Grace of Christ - Service through Worship

V THE MISTS DISPERSE 45
Neither Death nor Separation - Man earns for himself Heaven or Hell - Longing for God

VI A CLEAR AND GOLDEN SKY 55
Right Thought - All-Enfolding Love You are never alone - Inner Worlds Break your Bonds - Brotherhood - Rise in Spirit

Title page of MORNING LIGHT *with (below) the more expensive publications of 1955. The new policy bore immediate fruit for the White Eagle Publishing Trust, for 1958 saw* MORNING LIGHT *become the very first White Eagle book in translation, in Dutch. There have since been translations into languages as wide apart as Slovak, Japanese and Turkish.*

ulated this desire to serve. There was an increasing awakening to the power of good thought and of the work with the Light which White Eagle had been teaching for so many years: also, the work of the Brotherhood had become known through some of the books. Thus, as people became attached to the Lodge and to the White Eagle path, many felt the call to dedicate themselves wholly to this inner service under the magic of the Star. Before 1957, only those living close enough to a Lodge to be able to attend it regularly were eligible for it. White Eagle's guidance that an 'outer' circle of the Brotherhood should be called together meant that this work was open to all who proved themselves to be truly dedicated: an opportunity to any member, even if he or she lived on the other side of the world, to become part of the great chain of Brotherhood which does indeed now stretch round the world. The first initiations into this special work took place on 11 March, and ever since the band of Outer Brothers, now known as Star Brothers, has grown steadily.

On the publishing side, a contribution to the twenty-first birthday was the issue of a bibliography of all the White Eagle publications, starting with THE HEAVENS ARE RINGING, Brother Faithful's story of the Burstow ghost, published in 1930. But the most significant event of 1957 was the launch of what was called 'the Cheap Book Series', beginning with MORNING LIGHT. The conception was Geoffrey Hayward's. Conscious of the high cost of producing a book – the most recent, THE RETURN OF ARTHUR CONAN DOYLE, a revised edition of THY KINGDOM COME,* commemorating the twenty-first birthday, had had to sell for rather more than our own members or most Spiritualists could easily afford – he looked for ways of producing a pocket hardback book which could sell for as little as the MORNING LIGHT cost when it appeared. In 'in old money' (and it scarcely translates today), MORNING LIGHT cost five shillings, only a third of the price of the Conan Doyle book. The conception also was to produce a book complete in itself in which extracts from White Eagle's teaching were grouped around a particular theme or for a particular purpose. This was an instruction White Eagle himself had given us: a book which would help those starting on the spiritual path (this was MORNING LIGHT); another, which looked towards what lies at the end of that path (GOLDEN HARVEST, published in 1958); and a third, describing the higher worlds, for those afraid of death particularly, or affected by bereavement (SUNRISE, 1958). Later HEAL THYSELF was added to the series (1962) and finally the bedside book of White Eagle readings, THE GENTLE BROTHER (1968).

Looking back on these publications, we realise what a revolution

*It has changed again! The present edition carries the title ARTHUR CONAN DOYLE'S BOOK OF THE BEYOND. MORNING LIGHT is now FIRST STEPS ON A SPIRITUAL PATH, while GOLDEN HARVEST is LIVING WITH LOVE. THE GENTLE BROTHER continues as PRACTISING PEACE. HEAL THYSELF and SUNRISE are unchanged.

they represent. Breaking away from the old style of book – the large collections of teaching – they gave an enhanced feeling of light and clarity and have formed the pattern for a great many of our books since then. They also proved valuable sources of readings in churches and for groups inside and outside the White Eagle Lodge. This, along with the price, led to increased sales as hoped, which in turn gave opportunities for further expansion. They thus formed the foundation of the huge increase in sales of all the books in the 1960s and 1970s.

The feeling of 'light and clarity' arose from another aspect of the books besides the editing, that of design. Although we look at the very early White Eagle books with great pleasure – we were very fortunate with our early illustrators and printers, and some of the books have a pleasing 'Arts and Crafts' feel to them – this kind of production was quite uneconomical in the fifties, if indeed it was even possible. With the War, standards had fallen badly and although considerable effort was spent on MEDITATION and HEALING in 1955, it was the Cheap Book Series that really provided the new standard. Geoffrey's design used a large and attractively individual typeface on a smallish page with good margins. All was neatly done, and the book was bound in a cream-coloured imitation vellum and wrapped in cellophane to give it a sparkle (this tended to get damaged and was eventually replaced by a paper jacket).

In the new wave of publications another brother may be mentioned. Keith Ellis worked with a large East Anglian book printer, and was so stirred by the poor appearance of one of the early post-war books, he offered his services when appropriate. It was another instance of someone being sent at just the right time. Not only did his advice open up new possibilities, it also enabled us to save money while actually increasing quality. As STELLA POLARIS informed its readership,

> We have recently completed the preparation of a geographical posting list. This means that we now have the names and addresses of all our members and friends not only listed alphabetically but also grouped together in a separate index under the countries and counties and towns in which they live. Of course we never divulge a name or address without the owner's permission, but this new index means that we can now more easily link you with other friends in your neighbourhood should you be interested in forming a group for the study of White Eagle's teaching.
>
> *February–March 1957*

This was a more mundane event than the other events of 1957 but one which probably contributed more than any other single factor to the growth of the group work all over the world in the decade fol-

Christmas Fair in the London Lodge, 1962, a photograph taken from the gallery above

lowing. The remark about confidentiality sounds quaint in today's world of Data Protection but it has always been a strict guiding principle with us.

Not a great deal has been said to date about the healing work, growing quietly but steadily through the years. By 1959 the original two absent healing groups had grown to forty or more, a number which included thirteen groups sitting on their own in other parts of the country. Through all the early years the contact healing was given entirely by individual healers in private chapels. Joan, for whom this side of the work had always been her special care, later described White Eagle's masterly handling of each patient who came for diagnosis (before receiving treatment). 'He seemed to look right into their hearts and by his love to melt away the fears and conflicts which beset them and were of course the basic cause of the physical inharmony.'

In 1954 these private sessions were replaced by a monthly healing service conducted by White Eagle, when first he spoke generally and then gave individual diagnoses to about six patients, allotting them healers there and then, with full instructions for their treatment. This monthly healing meeting developed into a service for the laying-on of hands, taken by White Eagle. At these services he gave a talk to patients and healers, and at a certain point the patients were called forward and the healers treated them by just holding their hands above the patient's head.

In 1959 and under White Eagle's guidance the contact healing work was reorganised into roughly its present form. The monthly service and the private treatments were replaced by a daily healing service at which the patients were treated by White Eagle's colour method according to their individual needs.

With this change came another, for the monthly healing service became the service of communion and dedication, purely for Lodge healers, which remains an essential part of the White Eagle healing work and means so much to us all. People find them 'oases of blessing and refreshment, from which the participants emerge recharged and inspired to keep on keeping on faithfully with their loving service to humanity' (Retrospect 1960).

Retrospect 1960 (that is, the Newsletter published in 1961) also announced the launch of the Lone Healing programme.

> For some years now a few members who were prevented by circumstances from sitting in an absent healing group at one of the Lodges have been linking in to certain groups as absentee sitters. As the numbers of those longing to serve in this way are growing, we are guided to form a special group for 'Lone Healers', which will give to those of you who feel cut off from the Lodge activities a chance to serve in a unique way, at the day and time of your own choice. If you would like to become a 'White Eagle Lone Healer' please write to the Secretary for further particulars.

It was a milestone indeed in the White Eagle service, for the lone healing work now stretches across the world.

It was in this Newsletter (the healing planets must have been shining brightly) that we printed an appeal White Eagle had made,

> There will be a period of silent communion and prayer (at New Lands) every day until there is a spiritual atmosphere, a holy centre of power to which all may come and really touch and see and know God. This is the purpose of the work, the building up of the invisible life-force which will be like a great fountain blessing all souls who are guided here by the invisible Brotherhood whom you serve.
>
> So now, not only on Christmas morning but every morning at twelve o'clock, this call to communion in the chapel at New Lands goes out and those who are on the estate at the time answer the call. We believe you will like to think of this ever-burning light at New Lands and that you will sometimes join us in spirit at these times to give and to receive the blessing.

Minesta and Brother Faithful with Rosemary and Paul Beard, their companions on the trip to the Pyrenees referred to on p. 53

Thus it was that the twelve-noon call to prayer and to send out the Light, which had been such a feature of the early wartime era, was reborn in our Silver Jubilee year, and is today observed by followers of our teaching all over the world. The little light on the altar at New Lands never goes out, it is a constant flame.

At the purely material level, the mortgage debt on New Lands was finally cleared before the Silver Jubilee celebrations. And also by the generosity of members three improvements were made at St Mary Abbots Place, reported by Minesta in her 'Chain of Fellowship' for December 1961. One, the installation of adequate oil heating, at last, so that 'the Lodge will henceforth be cosily and cleanly warmed throughout'. Two, new wood-block flooring: 'For how many years have we all endured with exemplary stoicism, cold feet and shivering backs, due to the damp rising through the cold stone floor! Now all will be warm and dry'. Three, a new central chandelier for the main chapel. It need hardly be said that all three gifts were, quite literally, warmly appreciated.

CHAPTER IV

The Temple

How can we measure the progress of a spiritual work such as this? Not by the numbers and publicity it attracts. Progress is measured by the effect on every individual life that the light of the Lodge reaches – here or on the other side of the world. All who come into the White Eagle Lodge to worship and to serve must grow in the inward grace, or in inward power to affect the lives of others....

The purpose of our work here is that every soul who enters the Lodge, every soul who participates in the work, shall grow in spiritual power, which will radiate from him to give light and healing to the world. Remember – it is not what comes from the lips, but from the heart, which can inspire a life with love and joy and peace. The White Eagle work should be as leaven in the bread of life to the world.

White Eagle

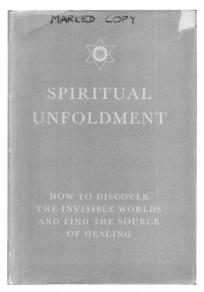

Battered cover of an editorial copy of SPIRITUAL UNFOLDMENT 1. *Another publication from 1961, it formed the first of a 'second series' of books on spiritual unfoldment that is at the centre of our publishing list still today.*

STELLA POLARIS for April 1961 has a simple silver cover with the title picked out in blue and our rose-star symbol above it. Beneath are the words 'The White Eagle Lodge Silver Jubilee'. Twenty-five rather eventful years of Lodge history had gone by, and the Lodge had come out of them with an identity very close to what it has today, despite the enormous growth that has occurred since; rather as a person's character is moulded in adolescence but shows more clearly in the twenties, when the soul becomes fully incarnated.

We marked the Jubilee with a special service – some of White Eagle's words then have been given elsewhere in this book (pp. 11, 158) – and also with a merry party at the London Lodge, held on the very anniversary itself, 22 February 1961. 'The first thing that we all saw as we entered the Lodge', says the account in STELLA POLARIS, 'was the great silver star against the dark blue background of the curtains, with silver rays reaching down to meet the glorious display of flowers and greetings arranged below'. Our Brother 'Mark', Paul Beard, proposed a toast, comparing the Lodge to 'a broad, great big sheltering oak tree'. Brother Faithful picked this up in his reply, and reminded us of the strength of an oak. But the strength, he said, lay in the devoted service given by members and friends of the Lodge. 'I do not undervalue the financial, the material help – that indeed has been generous and kind; but the most precious gift anyone can give is their life for the White Eagle work; their constant service, their love, their sympathy, their friendship'. But it is to Minesta's own speech that we turn particularly:

> When this Lodge was called into being, White Eagle said: 'You build on the four-square'. Well, there happened to be just four of us in the family at that time. But he meant far more than four-square people. The four-square base is perfect…. And we must remember to apply this … to our dealings with our fellow men and women: be always on the square, be true and straight…. From the four-square base – right living, right thought, right speech, right action – comes the pyramid of spiritual Light, the development of the spirit. And then the spirit sees the vision of the perfect six-pointed star-symbol of the Christ-man, or the perfected soul. I would like to hold this symbol before you all. May every one of us pray to have the strength and the vision to act and live and serve on the square.

This is a message equally apposite after more than seventy years of work today.

The family had indeed been four, and with John Hodgson and Geoffrey Hayward it had increased to six, but the following year the number of the family involved in the running of the Lodge rose to seven with the first of the next generation, Rose, entering the work as Minesta's personal secretary – as well as taking on the cooking for the retreat weeks at New Lands, a job which cannot have seemed more than a humdrum task at the time, but which was to have remarkable consequences! Rose, only 17 at the time, had her sights on university and cannot have foreseen what the change of plan would lead to. She became engaged that same year, to Anthony Elliot, the son of 'Mary' and 'John', leaders of the Plymouth Lodge, and they were married in the London Lodge on 24 August 1963.

This period is also marked by important developments in the healing work and in the running of the Lodge. For a long time, the only secretarial help we had had was that of the irreplaceable Alison Innes, Sister 'Pearl', as a personal assistant (and also as the most meticulous of proofreaders), and of Margaret Ross, a remarkably capable secretary, who ran the General Office (with our staff of today it is incredible to think of the clerical work, including the typing and duplicating of White Eagle's weekly teachings, being done by one person).

Late in 1960, however, we took on in addition Isobel Hutchings, whose assistance made possible a major reorganisation of the absent healing administration. At this time there was developed a system

The house 'Gwyn Mennay', home of the Plymouth Lodge under Mary and John Elliot, early 1960s; Minesta and Brother Faithful are visiting

of maintaining proper reports on patients' progress, and an efficient system of adhesive slips by which patients could be added to the healing lists. It seems primitive today, but was revolutionary then!

Very influential in these changes were some of our brothers who were drawing close to help the work. Rosemary and Paul Beard suggested several of the improvements, and Peter and 'Billie' Hamilton (Moonflower, as everyone has known her) dealt with some of the correspondence with patients. Other brothers helped in typing lists, and with the Lone Healing. But the greatest contribution of the brothers we have mentioned was in the day-to-day running of the London Lodge, where Peter and Moonflower and Paul and Rosemary, each as a pair, took charge for individual days of the week and enabled Minesta's family to devote more time to the country centre. Paul also looked after the fabric of the building with a professional's eye.

One of whom special mention must be made is Sister 'Radiance' (Irene Hancock) for her links, so far as this incarnation are concerned, go back to the days before even the Lodge started. Her wartime work as Private Secretary to an important Cabinet Minister limited the amount she was able to do in those early years, but after the War she gave more and more time to White Eagle.

In 1948 she came to live in one of the flats in 9a St Mary Abbots Place and during succeeding years her work in the London Lodge built up to the point where she was taking overall care, as the family became increasingly involved at New Lands. The extent of her contribution to the work, in loving and selfless service in many different ways and at all levels, would be impossible to overstate. So many came to know and love her over the years and turned to her as a friend in need, and they will join us, we know, in paying loving and thankful tribute to her at all stages of her life and commitment to White Eagle.

Another great server was Sister 'Peace' (Enid Brown) who took early retirement from her career to devote herself wholly to the Lodge work. In the early 1960s she completely reorganised and reclassified the London Lodge library and set it on much the same footing it has today. Today her spirit presence is still with us and many have felt an unseen hand guiding them as they use the library. Another sister, 'Serena' (Marian Bumford), recorded White Eagle's Sunday Addresses meticulously for more than twenty years and our debt to her is considerable.

There were many, many others, of course, for the work was growing all the time – willing helpers whose work and devotion are built into the very fabric of the Lodge. It is not possible to name them all, but in our hearts they will always be remembered.

A time of growth and a time of loss, which paradox was never so particularly felt as in 1965. On 2 March, Rose gave birth to

'Peter'; 'Radiance'; 'Peace'

Katharine, her first daughter and Minesta's first great-grandchild. But in January 'Mark' (Paul Beard) left us to give a decade of his life to the administration of the College of Psychic Studies in South Kensington.* Two months later Geoffrey Hayward's destiny took him away from the family group and from the running of the Lodge, after he had endowed it with the deep gifts of his vision – and of his own practical ability, in the production of books.

At this time also there had come into the work Jenny, fresh from school and college, and she started by taking on much of the responsibility which Rose, with a young child, was now unable to carry. To Jenny's charm we owe the help, over a crucial period, of Stuart Neil, who took on some of Geoffrey Hayward's responsibility for the running of the 'business' of the Publishing Trust (and in the process reformed its accounting and stock control systems); he will come back into this story later. To Jenny we also owe the bringing of Geoffrey Dent full-time into the work in 1972. It was he who permanently took on the business management of the Publishing Trust, and who helped to lighten John (Hodgson) of his huge load with the Lodge accounts, eventually becoming Treasurer of the Lodge in 1979. Geoffrey and Jenny were married in the London Lodge on 11 April 1970.

Perhaps this awareness that a new generation was emerging is also symbolised in Joan's book WHY ON EARTH, which was published in 1964. Written at the request of, and partly financed by, the 'Eaglets', it was originally to be entitled 'Light on the Hills' (the much punchier title was suggested by John) and carried the subtitle 'The Light of the Ancient Wisdom on Modern Problems'. It thus formed an introductory book about White Eagle's teaching, and at the same time drew on the teaching to give a moral lead in the permissive 1960s. It was much revised in 1978.

37 Pompstationsweg, The Hague: from October 1965, a special destination for many years!

HOLLAND, THE HAGUE. Saturday, October 16th, 1965, was indeed a memorable occasion for the Dutch Group at The Hague. On this day White Eagle spoke to over fifty people at the dedication ceremony. More had wished to attend but could not be accommodated in this beautiful sanctuary. All day long flowers had arrived from friends in Holland and in England, bringing their own message of love; and blessing, both for this centre and for White Eagle.

STELLA POLARIS, December 1965–January 1966

The Dutch Lodge was the second overseas Daughter Lodge and was largely the result of the tireless efforts of its leader, Margaret

*Paul returned to the London Lodge after his retirement and was a regular attender of the Brotherhood until very shortly before his death at the age of 97, in 2002.

Petri-Moora. White Eagle spoke memorably on this occasion, which was the first time Minesta had travelled overseas on Lodge business, and marked in a general way the beginning of an era. There was a significant growth in the number of Daughter Lodges in the early 1960s with Worthing, Ascot and Reading also joining those of the 1940s (Edinburgh, Glasgow and New Jersey) and 1950s (Bournemouth and Plymouth).

These developments in the worldwide work are an indication of a general expansion in the 1960s which has continued. Undoubtedly one of the catalysts later in the decade was the launch of the Affiliation Scheme in 1966. This was designed to enable independent groups of servers to associate themselves with the White Eagle family, but its chief effect was to encourage individuals to start White Eagle groups, either to do their healing work with others, or to provide opportunities for discussion and meditation. Affiliation remains the first step towards the eventual establishment of a fully-fledged White Eagle Group or larger centre.

1966 was a momentous year, partly because of the Affiliation Scheme, and partly because of an extensive restructuring of the London Lodge that was completed late that year. Although the

Dedication of the Dutch Lodge (above). Below, the Reading Lodge was created on 24 April 1962. The picture shows founders Betty Jones and Leo Lane, at a London Lodge gathering

THE STORY OF THE WHITE EAGLE LODGE

main chapel, Brotherhood Chapel and present library have been little altered over the years (though the library has been both sitting room and chapel), most of the other rooms, in shape and in use, date from the building works of 1966. But the main reason for the significance of 1966 lies elsewhere.

At the Thirtieth Anniversary Service White Eagle spoke as usual, but Sir Arthur Conan Doyle came very close too, we are sure, and he seemed to give the service special power. White Eagle however kept his surprise for us till the end of his message:

> Now, turn your mind to our centre in the country, to New Lands, which stands on the hill. Upon that hill we are holding in thought, we see being built in the ether, a simple but pure temple through which will flow increasing heavenly wisdom and power – which will become a centre of life, a centre of light.
>
> We therefore charge all our brethren, all members and friends, to come in and help us to erect our temple on the hilltop, just as the temples were built in ancient days, which served their purpose, though they have now crumbled away. This temple has a still greater purpose to serve, long after those of you here will be with us in the spirit. This must be your gift, and our gift to coming generations.
>
> *Reprinted in* STELLA POLARIS, *June–July 1966*

What a charge! Yet it was not one for which White Eagle's family were totally unprepared. The story, told by Ivan Cooke in THE TEMPLE ANGEL, seemed to go back to their first years at New Lands.

> Minesta had had a dream then, in which she was led to a monastery in Italy, overlooking the Mediterranean. A monk in a white habit, whom she knew to be a saint of the early Christian Brotherhood, greeted her, and pointed up the hill before them, as if indicating 'that there were greater heights to climb and more work still to be done for the Brotherhood'. The dream remained with her. In 1965, at the instigation of a brother of the Lodge, Minesta and Faithful set off to Italy to find the monastery. Finding it by a happy piece of guidance, she was again visited by the saintly monk.
>
> We were told that the work had come to a point of change, and fresh power and inspiration were needed. We had been brought here for this purpose to give us further insight into the plan. A new phase was coming into the work of the White Eagle Lodge, greater power, more revelation, further proofs. We were given further insight into the Star Brotherhood, its power and its light. We were shown a vision of the inner meaning of the brotherhood of all life, not only of brotherhood between men on earth,

but the brotherhood of men and angels, the brotherhood of men with nature, with the solar life. We were told that through the past twenty-five years we had been upheld and maintained by the power of the Star, waiting for the time when further progress was to be made toward the establishment of the Star Brotherhood on earth.

Referring to the work at New Lands, it was said that New Lands would become an unusual and powerful spiritual centre, and that a new chapel, or temple, was to be built on the hill. It would be world-known in the years to come.

Ivan Cooke, THE TEMPLE ANGEL

This was the first clear intimation given to Minesta about the Temple, but it is apparent to us now that the Brothers in spirit had held the plan for many earthly years. We recall, for instance, some of White Eagle's words to Minesta's family on New Year's Eve in 1944, the occasion on which he told them about New Lands. The full significance of his words, however, can hardly have reached them.

White Eagle had said:

It will be in the year 1945 that a light will be lighted in the history of the White Brotherhood, of the White Eagle Lodge. You will lay the foundation in this year upon which will be erected a pure White Temple which will live, which will remain standing and which will expand and grow in influence long after you have left your present body.... It is a work with a small beginning, but a vast future. We foresee, we hope, that the chapel will be a place of meditation, a meeting place between heaven and earth.

Reprinted in Newsletter, February 1966

But there is an even more remarkable story to tell, for it goes back well before the Lodge itself came into being. We have written already of Mabel Beatty's circle, which Minesta was invited to join in 1930. Records of Mrs Beatty's circle from April that year to January 1931, during which period White Eagle spoke on most occasions, remained forgotten until we began work on this book. But we find that on 4 April 1930 Minesta, in semi-trance, gave a message that must, at the time, have been rather an enigma. Her words were:

We tell you again that one is coming to you from across the water – one who has great knowledge and wisdom – he is coming to you. [This must be a reference to the Polaire messenger.] I can see a white building which will stand in London. No – not London – but [the] foundation is in London. The white building is peaceful and quiet.

Truly a remarkable prophecy.

*

And so a new period of fundraising began.

We had only just recovered from a dry rot outbreak in the London Lodge, but were soon busy collecting our first 'million sixpences' for the Temple building fund. Joan's daughter Rose was engaged on another project as well. Over the twenty years New Lands had been run as a retreat centre, we had accumulated quite a collection of vegetarian recipes, all tried and tested and with the New Lands stamp. White Eagle has always advocated progressive change to a vegetarian diet (it was Rose herself, in childhood, who finally brought the family off fish) and had given us a vision of a time to come, not so far in the future, when no one will eat meat. Indeed, in 1970 he stated prophetically that in the next decade people would turn to vegetarianism because there wouldn't be enough meat to feed them – something borne out by the growing realisation now that only crops, not livestock, use land sufficiently economically to be feeding the world.

At this time, two New Lands brothers, Peter and Edna (later Anna) Roberts, felt moved to start an organization promoting greater awareness in agriculture of the needs of animals and of the soil. Compassion in World Farming was formed in 1967 and Minesta and Faithful were two of its founder-Trustees. It is now a leader in its field and has been enormously influential in bringing about improved conditions for farm animals, first in the UK and later internationally.

Rose too took up the challenge of White Eagle's words about a meatless diet, for we all felt that the Lodge had a part to play in facilitating the great change of attitude that was to come. Experimenting, adding her own genius and easy literary style to the recipe ideas worked out for the retreats, she produced a cookbook, SIMPLY DELICIOUS, also in 1967. It was an entirely new venture for the Publishing Trust, and no one was quite prepared for the success it had. Five years later Rose wrote NOT JUST A LOAD OF OLD LENTILS (the title arose from a chance remark to the book's illustrator, in a shop), which was the book eventually spotted by Fontana. Today Rose has over sixty different cookbooks to her name (and one on astrology, following in her mother's footsteps!), and she must have done as much as any writer in Britain to promote the image of vegetarianism.

Rose's books had an important effect on our development, for they introduced New Lands and the Lodge to a much wider circle. Many members today owe their introduction to SIMPLY DELICIOUS, which in its first full year of publication sold as many copies as all our titles put together had sold only three years previously. We were also producing books regularly, at least one new one every year and

Picture of Rose taken for SIMPLY DELICIOUS

sometimes two. Overall book sales rose from a steady 3000 in the early 1960s to over 10,000 by 1970. Yet those increases pale beside those of the 1970s, which have a different cause.

Ever since the first bulk order of ILLUMINATION was despatched to New York in the 1930s, sales of the books in the U.S.A. had been growing, and by the early 1970s we had two distributors taking several thousand copies between them. Then we lost them both – and gained another, De Vorss of California. Though our relationship began slowly, it soon 'took off' and today the number of books sold in the U.S.A., through De Vorss and elsewhere, is huge.

Just prior to this – in 1972 – we produced a book of White Eagle's teaching which, quite unexpectedly, was a breakthrough in getting White Eagle's message through to the general public. As an indication of its success in this, within a few years some of the passages in the book were reprinted in a U.S. Navy chaplaincy prayer book, a collection for use in prisons, and in a devotional collection produced by one of the English universities, and institutionally in the care of the dying. We leave Ylana to tell the story of THE QUIET MIND.

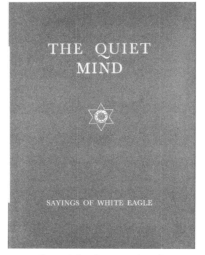

'Every White Eagle book has its own memories, but THE QUIET MIND particularly stands out because of the way its compilation was, in effect, taken out of my hands. The popularity of White Eagle's Calendar and the great help it was proving to its readers suggested that a book of his collected sayings would be valuable. It sounds easy enough, but you can't just throw "sayings" together haphazardly – and how to arrange them in any sort of order? I tried this way and that for days but nothing seemed right, and I began to despair and feel the book wasn't "on". I went to sleep one night with a prayer in my heart for guidance. Next morning I woke early with an inner voice saying "The secret of strength lies in the quiet mind….". I knew immediately that "The Quiet Mind" was the title and that White Eagle was leading me to the passage in MEDITATION which begins with those words.

'I read the passage, found it fell beautifully into headings; went to my work table where all the White Eagle sayings were laid out, and in no time at all they were sorted under those headings – and from the hundreds of sayings the right ones seemed to present themselves and fall into order. By lunchtime, the task was complete, apart from writing the introduction, and my heart was singing!'

By 1980, sales of the religious books had risen to over 55,000 per annum, with the vegetarian books accounting for another 13,000 (by this time we were already running down our distribution of cookery books, as larger publishers could obviously do it more effectively than we could). By that same time, as many as sixty per cent were sent overseas. Many of these were to the U.S.A., but the sales in Australasia were also large and we had distributors in South Africa and Nigeria. In the despatch of these books we must record (among oth-

Its original, very simple cover announces that our most popular book ever published sells for 40p

Work week, despatching a mailing: the team includes (left) Eileen Thompson, (behind) Arthur Higgins, and London's 'three musketeers': Vyvienne Young, Ethel Cooper and Anne Brooks

Ellie and Basil Gillam, whose group became the first Sydney White Eagle Daughter Lodge

ers) the service of Charles Waters, our Brother 'James', who retired at the age of 80 in 1973, having seen his job grow from the packing of four or five thousand books a year to about 40,000! In other countries the translations boost the dissemination of the White Eagle teachings very considerably, particularly in Germany and Switzerland where the tireless work of two Brothers, Walter and Edith Ohr, brought about a very wide distribution of the books, later taken on by Peter Michel and Aquamarin Verlag. Their effort is mirrored in other countries where friends laboured to bring out translations of the books: Sweden, France and Holland especially. White Eagle books are now translated into most major European languages and we thank all who have made this work part of their service.

During the 1970s there was a comparable expansion in the membership of the Lodge. Our first annual newsletter, in 1955, referred to 376 members, of whom only 163 lived so far away they could not attend the London Lodge. In February 1966, our newsletter recorded 694. By 1973, the figure had doubled to 1536; and it doubled again to reach the 3000 mark in 1980. The regional groups grew in number similarly. There were 29 groups and Lodges in 1964. The affiliation scheme brought 14 new groups in its first two years; and by 1974 there were 80 groups in all – but 107 in 1978 and 132 in 1982. Daughter Lodges were established in Teignmouth in 1971, in Crowborough in 1975, and in Ipswich in 1976. Our Brisbane, Australia, Lodge dates from 1976 but had a forerunner in Epping, N.S.W., from 1968 to 1973.

This huge expansion meant an equally sudden expansion in the workload, and our memories of the late 1960s and 1970s are dominated by coping with the numbers – at all levels.

First among these numbers are those we had to fit into New Lands Chapel for Sunday services before the Temple was built. Any festival service involved chairs and a public address system in New Lands lounge, and on occasion in the hall and dining room as well. Then there was the huge number of advertising leaflets for the books which had to be printed. In those days, many more magazines than now took loose-leaf insertions, and as a Brother had made us a gift of the cost of a small offset printing machine in 1965 (in its effects, one of the more revolutionary gifts we have received), we were – workload apart – ideally placed to print literally hundreds of thousands of leaflets. Colum and Jeremy remember many school holidays with their hands blue with printing ink!

Lastly, there were those million sixpences – and more! – to be raised to build the Temple. When White Eagle gave us his vision it seemed daunting financially. But if we raised a million sixpences, as we had twice raised a million pennies (Britain was still using pounds, shillings and pence until 1971), we would be well on the way to paying for the Temple; and as he had said, maybe for every sixpence

A UK DAUGHTER LODGE ROUND-UP

The pictures show (top left) the sanctuary at Inverleith Row, in Edinburgh, many years ago; (top centre) the main chapel in the Reading Lodge at Erleigh Road, 1970s; (above) Minesta and family visit the Worthing Lodge, probably 1960s. Sister Felicia, Eve Wilson, stands on Brother Faithful's right. Below left: the Crowborough Group in 1975, just before it became the Crowborough Daughter Lodge (Jean LeFevre, with dog, at right); and the Ipswich Lodge in 1995, with Jenny and Geoffrey Dent visiting and John Kemp, tireless leader of the Ipswich Lodge, seated back right.

that we on earth put in, they in spirit would put in two. This really is how it was all through those seemingly endless days of fundraising; every time we counted the total of an individual campaign or fundraising event, it always seemed a bit bigger than we'd expected. Almost the whole sum of the Temple Fund was made up of small amounts. Not all of them were sixpences, but 'T.M.S.F. (K.O.K.O)', the mystic initials that the Eaglets gave the fund, symbolise it all: 'The Million Sixpence Fund (Keep On Keeping On)'!

Members, groups and Lodges organised numerous fundraising events – coffee mornings, evening parties, raffles and concerts; the children at New Lands held a sponsored silence; and individuals painted pictures, or sold crafts; we collected stamps, coins, anything! But no idea has had quite such a lasting effect as the sponsored walk, which was instituted in 1970 and became an annual event at Michaelmas. Always intended as a day on the Downs in the fresh air first, and a fundraising activity second, it nonetheless snowballed (to borrow a term from the one type of weather we never have had on the walk!) and it has been one of the most successful ways of raising funds. Much tribute is due to all who braved blisters and bruises for the Appeal; and to those whose sponsorship was always a sacrifice, however small or great.

We are very proud of the generosity of our members, and to have raised (in all the many ways we have described) over £140,000 in ten years until the cost of the Temple was paid off, was a wonderful achievement.

In all the fundraising, the younger generation took the lead in organising events and producing ideas. But there is one of them whose contribution to the building of the Temple was a very special one: Anthony Elliot (today he prefers to be called Robert) who came into the work in 1969. Anthony had first given us the benefit of his technical knowledge when the major reorganisation of the London building was carried out in 1966. He also inspired us to promote the Lodge teaching more widely, drew us our Lodge symbol, and drafted the longrunning 'Blue Star leaflet' about the Lodge. He saw into print the eight booklets about our teaching which are still available ('A Brief Outline of White Eagle's Teaching', etc.) and he made an outstanding contribution to the work with his skilful recordings of White Eagle's talks, some of which he later produced as our first LP records – and our first tape cassettes. But the seven years he took off from his job at an electronics and defence company, Plessey, were principally to see through the building of the White Temple.

It was not an easy task, neither for Anthony nor any member of the family. The original architects' very imaginative plan had eventually to be dropped – it was just too radical. In rather difficult circumstances we turned to a Lodge member whose expertise as an architect had been proven in the design of two of London's thea-

Making a start: the Temple driveway under construction and, below, Elidir's design takes form under scaffolding

tres, Elidir Davies. White Eagle told us that the Brothers in spirit could work through Elidir; and blending the direct guidance given to us with the inspiration he himself received, Elidir produced the design of the Temple as it stands today. Anthony's task was to get this vision actually built, and it was perpetually made difficult by the very difficulties the firms of builders we employed got themselves into, bankruptcy included. A huge debt of gratitude goes to one particular member who in our hour of need supplied craftsmen of all kinds to get the outstanding interior works done in those last few months, weeks and days.

Painful birthpangs indeed the Temple had (coupled for us with the worry of raising such a huge sum), and it was a late birth, too, when with literally hours to spare it was ready for opening as Minesta entered her eighty-third year on 9 June 1974. A brother wrote:

Visitors to New Lands on this day had come from distant places overseas and throughout Britain. But we were surrounded by an even greater company of radiant beings in spirit – recent brothers of the Lodge and rank upon rank of brethren of past ages, and mingling with these shining ones planetary angels, their flaming brilliance rising in spirals of light to the sun.

Into this glorious assembly of universal brotherhood came the white-robed choir on earth, uniting all hearts in praise as they sang Bach's chorale 'Now let every tongue adore Thee'. And then the whole congregation rose in tribute as Mr and Mrs Cooke entered the Temple....

Behind the altar are hung long curtains of pale yellow, as if spun from the rays of the sun. They suffuse the Temple with glowing ethereal light. In the centre of the altar which itself seems made of light stands the simple grail cup filled with liquid gold, burning the eternal flame, and above, caught in some sunlit ray, the scintillating crystal star – truly a breathtaking vision of beauty.

Together, choir, congregation and celestial voices (for those with ears to hear) sang 'the Old Hundredth', arranged by Vaughan Williams: 'All people that on earth do dwell'. White Eagle, enfolding us in his loving presence, spoke the simple words of dedication of this first temple of the New Age ... and, as if in answer, a wonderful excerpt from Brahms' *Requiem*: 'How lovely are thy dwellings fair' was performed by the choir....

White Eagle spoke with great power, sounding the note of brotherhood – brotherhood on a cosmic scale, for the earth is part of an infinite universe; brotherhood of all life on earth through conscious co-operation between man and the angels, man and the natural kingdoms; brotherhood and peace among men, for we are all one in spirit. The key to this universal harmony is obedience to the law of love.

As our Gentle Brother so inspired our vision, the sun streamed across the downland, through the amethyst windows, bathing us all in light. A shower of rain had blessed the Temple and in the distant rumble of thunder we heard echoes of the voice of God. The elements had indeed shared in the consecration of our Sun temple.

What could follow but Parry's 'Jerusalem'?

Tenderly Mrs Cooke, looking so young and so lovely, brought us back to earth with her heartfelt words of thanks, on this her most joyous of birthdays. And she urged us all to go out into the world and create more Temples of Light to guide humanity into the new age.

STELLA POLARIS, August–September 1974

The opening in fact was done twice over! We had so many applications for tickets that after fitting 500 people in on 9 June, we had nearly as many more for a thanksgiving service a week later. Now it is with us, The Temple, a dream realised, a meeting place for two worlds; and no one could have been more profoundly thankful than Minesta, when at last the work of all those years was done. She wrote:

Anthony (Robert) Elliot, whose contribution supervising the Temple's construction was huge, chats at the opening to the broadcaster Martin Muncaster, who later made a TV programme about the building

Frequently I walk with my husband across the garden to the Temple, which is now a landmark over a wide area of the Hampshire countryside, and there we gaze at its beauty, paying homage to the bushes and trees already planted in the Temple garden. My heart is full of gratitude for this miracle – for indeed it is a miracle, accomplished as all so-called miracles are by the steady concentration upon the Great White Spirit (God) and the power which emanates from God which brings us all together as one. The Temple is a demonstration of what can be accomplished by co-operative effort, and by trust in God.

Grace Cooke, Newsletter 1975

One good friend of the Lodge was Maurice Barbanell (Barbie), Silver Birch's medium, who had known Minesta almost since his boyhood. Over the years the Lodge had drawn gradually further away from the movement of Spiritualism as Minesta had known it in her youth, for part of its work was to try to create – as it were – the new Spiritualism. Barbie had a profound love for and loyalty to 'the Guides' as they were known – those teachers from the other side of life who were giving their profound and practical teaching through their chosen instruments on earth. It was all part of the great breakthrough from the world of the spirit to awaken men and women to the reality and closeness of that world. Barbie loved White Eagle, and he loved and admired White Eagle's medium too; this respect

Opposite: Minesta and Brother Faithful at the Temple opening

Temple interior, facing East

and affection created a very valuable bridge between the Lodge and the movement over which he had so much influence. The opening of the Temple was a proud moment for Spiritualism as well as for the Lodge. In the spring following, this pride was expressed formally when Minesta – to her intense surprise – was awarded the title of 'Spiritualist of the Year' in recognition of her work.

*

It is tempting to allow one's focus to be dominated by the building of the Temple at this time, but of course much else was going on. In particular, important developments were occurring overseas. Last time we focused here on the work in the USA, for instance, it was to describe the little Daughter Lodge in the south of New Jersey, beside the coast. That did not survive the passing of its leaders, al-

Temple interior, facing West

though there was an active group in Long Beach, California (whose leader Mary Hershey had been married by Minesta and Brother Faithful in Edinburgh right back in 1952 – see the photograph on p. 47)! Loyal servers remained all round North America.

Then, in 1970, one of them made a protracted visit to New Lands, immersing herself in the teaching. She was called Anne Stine (Sister Blue Star), and she went back and worked with Olive Robinson, but became the official information point for the work there. From Anne the flame passed to Ilabelle Shanahan (pictured, as is Anne, on pp. 96–7, and on to Roma Valenzuela in 1979). We read in STELLA POLARIS of a retreat day in Arizona in May 1978, another in San Francisco the same month, and the first ever White Eagle retreat in Canada, at Mississauga on Lake Ontario.

The same article carries a report of the second retreat week to be held by the new Brisbane, Queensland, Daughter Lodge, of which we shall hear much more later and mentions other active White Eagle workers: June Billingham in Sydney and Lesley and Fred Jefferson in Melbourne. From people such as these were to spring Daughter Lodges in New South Wales and Victoria in the years to come. The article also mentions 'a happy report of our first White Eagle Open Day in South Africa, held in August at the home of Evelyn van Vloten, leader of the new group at Kloof, near Durban'.

But as well as in South Africa, there were attempts to get the work 'off the ground' in West Africa. One young man who had this work in his heart right back in the 1970s was a young man from Nigeria, studying in London who was initiated in 1980 as White Star of Nigeria. His earthly name was John Okonkwo, and although the enterprise in West Africa has been led by many others since, it is touching that he is still with us today, a formal Trustee of the work there. Another London member, Georgina Aggrey, fed a little study group in Kumasi, Ghana, with White Eagle books out of her own pocket, while Robert Addy began a group in Accra.

Back home, a few changes in the form of the activities in the main Lodges were taking place in the period after the Temple opened. With the Temple in use for services, a different pattern for use of New Lands developed, and we began to run short courses there as well as the long-established retreat weeks. The first Group Leaders' Conference was held in 1976 and it has since become a very regular event in one form or another. It has increased the worldwide bonds that unite the 'family' in brotherhood, to have so many of the groups represented together. A new Daughter Lodge in East Anglia opened that same year.

An alternative type of Sunday service was introduced in London in April 1979. It was partly a response to the fact that it was difficult to maintain the size of congregation every week in London after the Temple opened, and was to take place every fortnight as a smaller service upstairs in the Brotherhood Chapel. What happened ultimately was that it proved so popular we ran out of chairs! In the 'New Age Communion' as it was first called, music played an important part in raising the consciousness into what is ideally an act of worship in meditation.

Minds in and outside the Lodge were set on the expansion of the sort of 'New Age' ideas the Lodge had upheld since 1936. We participated by request in the second Festival for Mind, Body and Spirit, held at Olympia in May 1978, and continued to support it for many years while 'Mind/Body/Spirit' became a widespread bookshop classification in the UK for publications such as ours. We were running with the tide! We had concerts from people like Frank Perry and Tim Wheater, who led a percussionist revival and developed the use of Tibetan Singing Bowls as a 'New Age' instrument.

Outdoors, the Sponsored Walk that had begun as a Temple fund-

Retreats at Willomee, home of the Brisbane Daughter Lodge, just after 1980, and a children's yoga class in the little chapel there

A display Norwegian members put on at a later New Age Festival

THE STORY OF THE WHITE EAGLE LODGE

Sponsored Walk, near Amberley

Accra group

Retreat at New Lands, shortly after the Temple was built. The group includes Walter Ohr, first translator of the teaching into German, between his sister Trudi and wife Edith (back row, left) and in the front row Sister Peace flanked by Arthur Patrick from Crowborough and Eric Warrington, founder of the Stockport group.

raiser in 1970 became a regular part of our year and focused attention on a younger, fitter group within the membership. During the 1970s yoga became a strong part of Lodge 'practice', with classes in many Lodges. Joan, aways interested in the health of the body, initiated this, but it was contact with Jenny Beeken, then a London member but today Principal of the Yoga of the Heart School, a little later, that really allowed yoga to take off though the foundations were laid by others. Yoga has now a strong foundation in the Lodge, and classes and courses are held regularly. The study of astrology increased, as we shall hear shortly in more detail.

Our Sister Radiance, who for so long had looked after the London Lodge, moved to New Lands at the end of the 1970s (and, with characteristic energy, took on many new duties there). 'Moonflower', Sister Rose Light, whom we have already mentioned, bravely stepped into the gap she had left and took daily charge until she too retired in 1983. In the meantime the younger generation, both in the wider family and in the immediate one, started to take a greater role, not only in the services but also in visits to Lodges and groups at home and overseas (and at events like the London Festival, just mentioned!). Colum and Jeremy Hayward finished studies at Cambridge University and joined the Lodge full time at the end of the 1970s.

There were inevitably losses of members of the first generation of the Lodge, too. One who was much missed at New Lands was 'Uncle Frank' Wharhirst, Minesta's brother-in-law and one of the stalwarts of the early brotherhoods at New Lands after it opened. He passed in February 1977. White Eagle had called him Brother Courage and, nursing a First World War wound for around sixty years, he was most aptly named. He had married Minesta's sister Beatrice (Bea) and both had been initiated in 1938. Bea passed in 1958, so his courage was needed in long widowerhood too.

After the struggles and frustrations of the years the Temple was being built, Minesta found herself able to work with renewed energy after the opening, and she and Brother Faithful, both now in their eighties, were to be seen on the Temple platform each time there was a public service, giving the address or in Minesta's case serving as channel for White Eagle. But as a Michaelmas summer, once over, turns so quickly into autumn, Minesta's health broke suddenly in 1976. We remember above all the very last time White Eagle spoke in public. It was at a Healers' Dedication Service, and although no-one knew it at the time, it is clear with hindsight that White Eagle was as certain then that he knew what was happening as he was at the special communion service before the bombing. This is how he ended his talk.

Build your own bridge, and live with God, and the blessing of the Great White Spirit is with you all.

We will not say 'good night', nor 'good-bye'. We will say, 'God be with you always, as we shall be with you always".

That was in April. In June she had to cease her public work completely. Joan and Ylana were already handling virtually all of the day-to-day business of the Lodge, and after she passed they were to formalise what was already visible, by sharing the role of Mother of the Lodge.

The next years were ones of great testing for Minesta, for the family who cared for her, and for the work, which missed her sorely. She was diagnosed with slowly developing breast cancer, which afflicted her with much pain, and the treatment for the pain disorientated and frightened her. The arrival of Evelyn van Vloten from South Africa, entirely volunteering to repay her a debt of gratitude and attend her nursing care, marked a watershed in her illness, and she went from being very disturbed to a newfound acceptance and serenity almost overnight. If Evelyn's arrival was symbolic (White Eagle had appropriately called her Shining Star), it was another White Eagle Brother, Eunice Watson, aptly named Sister Love, who over the whole period organised and led a team of agency nurses, every one of whom brought love and true care; we pay them tribute. At least two became members of the Lodge.

As Minesta became ill, so Brother Faithful's grip on life also deteriorated. On 3 September 1979 she 'gently and peacefully laid down the burden of her physical body and went forward, as someone has said, into the "light and loveliness she has so richly earned" through her life of service and the warmth of her love' (STELLA POLARIS, October–November 1979). Brother Faithful lived, but half in the other world, for nearly two years more, passing on 28 July 1981, just before 9 p.m. Eunice had continued to nurse him faithfully, to the end. It was the eve of the wedding of Prince Charles and Lady Diana Spencer, and thus 'just before the first beacon was lit which was the signal for the lights to spring up in a chain of fires all over Britain' (STELLA POLARIS October–November 1981). How well, outwardly, those beacon fires symbolised the inner work Brother Faithful had done for most of his life: that of building the fire of love and brotherhood in people's hearts – especially in his own country of Britain.

Some time after Minesta passed on, Ylana wrote in STELLA POLARIS *an account of a meditation she had had.....*

A little while ago we had, in meditation, an experience which we would like to share with you if we may. After that first still contact which we make in the heart of the Star, we knew we had to 'come down' a little into what White Eagle calls the infinite and eternal garden. We were taken to Minesta's home in that garden. The picture was very clear indeed, and almost as real as the room in which we are sitting to write this letter to you. We were taken into what appeared to be her study, and there was a desk there, at an angle half facing towards the window, and we could see her sitting at the desk, writing and we think studying. We mentally asked, why, in that heavenly state, when communication, in any case, is by thought, would she need to sit and write? The answer came very quickly, and with her usual wise twinkle, that she still enjoyed putting her thoughts into words in writing! But it was more than that really, for we knew, as we looked, that we too could come and sit at that desk when we were wanting to communicate with any one of her White Eagle family and to help them, and that she would be with us and, in so far as we allowed, speak to you in this way.

But what most impressed us about the room was that one whole side was in the form of a big picture window. As we looked out of the window we found that we were looking onto a view of the White Temple, just across a valley and shining in the sunlight, though there was just a little haze about it which, together with the intervening valley, conveyed to my mind that it was on a different level of life. Such a beautiful view Minesta had from her home in the spirit world, through the picture window, and we enjoyed it with her. But as we looked we began to wonder, and we asked why, beautiful as it was, she could possibly want to sit looking at the Temple—especially as no doubt she could visit whenever she wished to do so. Then, for a moment, we were in her heart, feeling her love for each one of her 'family' all over the world, and we knew that because the Temple was the heart of the work it was through the Temple that she felt and held in her own heart the need of each one of the family. She was very anxious not to give the impression of being anything wonderful or superhuman. Just a mother who still cared very much for her family; and it was as though those who were in need of that mother comfort and guidance could come in spirit to the Temple (which is in heaven as well as on earth) and she would help as she used to do when on earth.

She was also very aware of everything that goes on in the Temple and at New Lands, holding it all in her heart and gently guiding it in the right direction when necessary. And then we could see how through the Temple the link was made with each Lodge—first the old home, the London Lodge, seemed to come gently into focus and she held that in her heart, and then the other Lodges and Groups and the Centres overseas, and the leaders and workers came into view as the need arose—but always with this beautiful view of the Temple shining in the sunlight. She told us once again how close the two worlds are and how she and Brother Faithful come and walk in the Temple and New Lands garden as they used to do, and greet and welcome their friends in this garden of reunion. We talked together a little and then the time came for us to withdraw and return to the earth consciousness, which we did very reluctantly. But the picture of Minesta's home and that beautiful room with the view of the Temple through the picture window remains and will always remain a vivid memory.

We have found it difficult to find adequate words to describe the experience but we hope that it may have conveyed a picture which gives her message too.

THE STORY OF THE WHITE EAGLE LODGE

CHAPTER V

Continuing Minesta's Work

MINESTA would not wish us to labour her qualities – this very story is a tribute to all that she did. But we will permit ourselves to observe one quality above all, her obedience and loyalty to the guidance of the spirit, whatever the cost to herself. Without such a quality, our work would never have started, could never have continued through the war years, and could never have come to the great flowering of the Temple in 1974. We will have to leave the reader largely to imagine the tributes that came from all sides, when first Minesta and then Brother Faithful passed on, for to do them justice would be a book in itself. Yet one of the ways in which people have always paid tribute to Minesta was by their support of the work, and this greatly affects her memorial. We remember how when once the work was direly in need of funds to pay a builder for urgent remedial work, exactly the right money arrived in the form of a previously unnotified legacy – £13,000 – but most significantly the donor, of whom there was not trace on our records, specifically said it was a thank you for help received from Minesta.

A material memorial to Minesta and Brother Faithful exists, created out of just such thankful faith as this. During the great expansion of the worldwide work in the 1970s, it became ever clearer that the combination of our General Office, the room containing the Addressograph machine, and the borrowed rooms in the cottages on the estate used as personal offices, were ludicrously inadequate. One by one New Lands bedrooms were requisitioned, and sheds and outhouses round the estate converted for offices. Even then, desks had to be used on a timeshare basis!

This was one problem. The other was that although the Temple was operating successfully, we had had, when it was built, to abandon a second stage of the project giving more ancillary accommodation: chapels for healing groups, a meeting room for visitors, and a room for Brotherhood use. This was now becoming a pressing need. For instance, the only way to give visitors tea after a service – and some of them came hundreds of miles to the Temple – was to go over to New Lands house, in all weathers, and serve it there. The same applied to the needs of the sitters on healing groups. Moreover, the Temple bookstall was cramped, pressure on cloakrooms excessive,

Opposite: the Temple as it looked before the extension was built

and the crowd after a large service impossible to fit into the tiny area of the Temple foyer.

When Minesta passed on, it was obvious that her friends would want to do something in her memory. Our first thought was for the rose garden – the 'garden of remembrance' we had long wanted, and to which White Eagle had referred in his vision of the Temple. But the other needs seemed to hang over us, and one day Ylana had a very clear message from Minesta. We had to get on with the twin projects we were considering right away, while the tributes were still being paid. 'First the offices, then the temple extension.' And so the Grace Cooke Thanksgiving Appeal was launched, including the funds that had already come in as spontaneous gifts in her memory.

The office extension to New Lands

The Appeal got off to a head start, compared with the Temple Fund, as it began with a legacy. Symbolically, this was a very good foundation, because it was the legacy of Minesta's brother-in-law Frank Wharhirst, whom we have just mentioned (p. 82). A large part of his life in his later years was New Lands, which he had attended cheerfully and without a break since the very early days, and it is very fitting that the foundation of the Appeal for the new buildings was the capital realised from Frank's house in Petersfield, which he left to the Lodge.

This legacy and a later one, from a Brother in the West Country, were to be among four larger sums received for the Temple extension. Another was a private gift, and another was a grant of £50,000 by a charitable trust on the condition that we would allocate a similar sum to match it. With interest realised, these sums represented just over half the total found. The rest of the Appeal came as individual donations – whether made directly, or subscribed through one of the fundraising activities held at the Lodge or by one of the provincial groups – or, for that matter, the overseas ones. Many such gifts came as tributes to Minesta and Brother Faithful; but in October 1981 the Appeal was relaunched as the Golden Jubilee Thanksgiving Fund, in the hope that we could raise the amount by Jubilee Year. And we did – all £471,000 of it!

One of the fundraising events we should like to mention was a sponsored mountain-climb: rather evocative, it seemed, of our work as a whole, not just of the sum to be raised. The idea was to climb all the mountains in Snowdonia over 3000ft high in the space of a weekend. Perhaps it is best summed up in the words of one walker to another, when like everyone else his companion was suffering severe knee pain: 'It's at this moment it becomes not just a physical challenge, but a spiritual one as well!' A challenge the walkers responded to, and having climbed all fourteen peaks, they raised over £4000 for the fund, the largest amount ever raised by a single Lodge event. It was also the most exciting challenge our young people had ever set themselves. We think we hear them saying that they

We like our offices! Wendy Collett in one of them

And the Temple extension grows apace!

themselves felt the better for responding to the challenge, too. The memories of that challenge are in lasting friendships.

All sorts of activities were tried in order to raise funds and we thank everyone for their inventiveness. There was a regular 'Appeal Page' in STELLA POLARIS which gave news of them all. One of the most attractive, though not always the most effective financially, was the series of concerts held in the Temple over these years. They brought to us, in addition to some of our own talented musicians, wonderful solo singers, choirs and instrumentalists.

Another great help in being able to build the two extensions by Jubilee Year was the fact that we had an offer from one of our Brothers to oversee the construction himself. This not only improved the quality of workmanship, but cut our bills as well, and there is much for which we are deeply grateful to our Brother 'Clement', Alex Ross (seen in the picture on p. 100). He was truly guided to leave his home and work in Glasgow, where he was an experienced quantity surveyor, in order to guide the building work. In the case of the New Lands extension, which finally opened in the spring of 1984, he personally saw everyone comfortable in their offices, and continued his responsibilities beyond the mere construction stage with both buildings.

We thank you, Alex, and your team. In our Newsletter that year was conveyed – to all who had given their contribution to the

building of the offices – the gratitude of 'the Brotherhood in the world of light, who, because of the increased order and harmony in the office accommodation, will be able to give more help and inspiration to those who are doing the work at a practical level'.

During this time, a whole new generation of White Eagle books were produced. Perhaps their special task is to emphasise how the higher worlds interrelate with this one. THE STILL VOICE (1981) is a book of White Eagle readings which lead into meditations, THE WAY OF THE SUN (1982, now WHITE EAGLE ON FESTIVALS AND CELEBRATIONS) talks about the great festivals of the year and how they are celebrated in the higher worlds; and JESUS TEACHER AND HEALER (1985) seeks to make real for everyone that most perfect and gentle brother in the spirit. The books have also succeeded in carrying the teaching to a still wider readership.

As we stated earlier, this was a time fore the younger generation to take on the responsibility of the longer-distance trips. For Jeremy and Colum it was a visit to Australia in 1983, while Jenny and Geoffrey had a long-planned visit to the States in 1984. Each of these visits was representative of the worldwide character our work had taken on. Much attention was focused at the time on the Americas and Australasia, where retreat centres, built on the New Lands model, were planned. The Australasian centre was to be built in the hills of the Great Dividing Range north of Brisbane, overlooking virgin country, making it a focus for the whole continent, including New Zealand (where the work was also growing). The retreats Colum and Jeremy led on this site, however, utilising the existing building (see photographs) followed the pattern of the existing Brisbane Lodge retreats, while giving them major opportunity to meet brothers and members in Australia—which they did, also, by travelling overland from Brisbane first down to Sydney and then on to Melbourne.

Jenny and Geoffrey had a rather different, and in many ways more groundbreaking trip. Jean and John LeFevre had left England and the Crowborough Lodge in the early 1980s to live in Texas and (taking with her a wealth of experience from Crowborough, the animal welfare movement and the Theosophical Society) to co-ordinate the work in the Americas. The first task, it seemed, was to get everyone together in the same place as far as possible. And so a major conference was proposed, at the YMCA centre in the Colorado Rockies, with talks and presentations to be given by Jenny and Geoffrey on behalf of the Mother Lodge, but also from the (by now) growing number of experienced group leaders in the Americas. Over 100 attended, and the Colorado Conference was one of the most demanding gatherings that have been held in the White Eagle work. Although some difficult feelings were aired and shared, it truly has proved the foundation for the whole structure of the work in the Americas since. The photograph from a Brotherhood retreat

Australian experience: the little chapel at Willomee, shared until the Temple there was built by Sunday services and stocks of White Eagle books; a game on the grass outside it; and (for fun) the original shack to which Minesta and Brother Faithful came in July 1923 when they emigrated to Western Australia, before the start of this book!

At the top, the huge gathering which was the Colorado Conference, 1984.

For greater ease in recognising faces, see the picture here of a follow-up retreat for Brothers in the group in Long Beach, California. Among those pictured are (back row, left, somewhat hidden) John and Jean LeFevre; (middle row, from left) Mary Hershey, Long Beach leader, Doris Hagermann, first group leader in Canada, and Anne Stine (see p. 79), while the figure bottom right is the young Ernie Paller, known later as Brother Lawrence. Full list on p. 158. Below, Jenny and Geoffrey Dent at the Conference.

in Long Beach the following year (1985) shows at least some of those who participated in the conference, and in almost every case the part they have played in the work since has been substantial.

The conference was also intended to pave the way for the development of a new centre for the work, near Houston, Texas, chosen partly for its centrality. Although the proposed retreat centre site was geographically the same as the new Montgomery Daughter Lodge (designated such in Jubilee Year, 1986) it would serve two continents, for we had groups in Mexico and Brazil already, as well as those in the U.S.A. and Canada. Although each had been chosen because of the locality of the Daughter Lodge, each was a special site in itself and had some of that feeling of inner power we have learnt to recognise.

In Golden Jubilee Year our own sponsored walk at New Lands was to be held in aid of these two projects on opposite sides of the world, and added to it there was to be a special eighty-mile pilgrimage walk to New Lands from the stone circle at Avebury, uniting our efforts at the Mother Lodge with those of the brethren in the New World and in the Southern Hemisphere and – hopefully – with the footsteps of ancient Sun brothers and sisters. Of this, more anon.

So, a generation had passed on, a great jubilee – our Golden Jubilee – was approaching, and the Lodge was still full of energy. Without Minesta, was it still vibrant; inspired; did White Eagle's teaching seem to run through every aspect of it still? Joan and Ylana, as new joint Mothers of the Lodge, along with the other writers of the 1986 edition of this book were able at this point to move into the present tense, and it feels appropriate to quote what was said as a statement of 'how we felt at the time of the Golden Jubilee' that year. All the remainder of this chapter is as it was written then, and has been reprinted unrevised; it should perhaps be reread at the end of this book, for it is a lovely 'envoi' that brings Minesta, Brother Faithful and White Eagle incredibly close.

'And so we come to the present moment, and to our future. We have just seen the Temple extension come into use, not in Jubilee Year, but actually in time to give shelter to the special events we have been holding in Jubilee Year. How, we can now ask ourselves, could we possibly have organised them otherwise? And yet we would not have dared think, when the Appeal was launched, that they could actually be built and paid for by the end of 1985.

'The Temple extension already has an atmosphere of its own, serene and somehow joyous too. Its centre (though not its geographical centre) is the Brotherhood Library, which includes books of the many religions of the world, many of them from Minesta's own collection, and houses the twelve-leaved round oak table (com-

Ceremony around New Lands dining room table in 1983, when all UK Daughter Lodge leaders signed a legal covenant with the Mother Lodge. Trustees Noel Gabriel and 'Radiance' (Irene Hancock) are also present. For fuller details, see p. 158

Table in the Brotherhood Library at the New Lands Temple, designed by Jon Barnsley and made at the Edward Barnsley workshop near Petersfield

missioned from the Edward Barnsley workshop nearby) which we find touches our spirits as well as our earthly senses with its beauty.

'Minesta asked me to give you this message and to ask you to open your vision and see that she is here in her gold robe. She comes with so much love for every one of you in this group, even if you do not know her.… White Eagle, too, you will see, so full of love, so radiant, and he asks us … to lift heart and mind to that beautiful Star.

'Now White Eagle and Minesta and the band behind them want you to know a very important truth: that for this group of the Lodge of the White Eagle something very important is happening. Minesta and Faithful, through the will of the Great White Spirit and under the direction of the shining Brotherhood, have to withdraw in their physical bodies, at the moment, from this work, but they work with us in spirit, and White Eagle wants everyone to realise the importance of this period when a bridge of light is being built.

Joan Hodgson, address in London Lodge, 7 August 1977

'Although these words were spoken two years before Minesta's passing, it would not be inaccurate to date the current phase in the White Eagle work from the time they were given. The nature of this phase is defined in the clause we have put in italics: 'a bridge of light is being built'. In other words, we are at a stage when our most important task is to show the closeness of the two worlds and to show how – without a psychic instrument – we all can be fully aware of those on the other side of life and of the help we receive from the advanced souls there. This has always been true of the Lodge work, but at the present time the passing of our founders and leaders, Minesta and Brother Faithful, gives us an unequalled opportunity to make this truth real.

'In our work the symbol of the Star has grown more and more real, as has the sense of oneness which comes with it. It is, truly, the way to the higher world. And the Temple, the earthly temple of the Star, is a place where the two worlds can meet. Increasingly, it has become a focus for workers for the Light. Many visitors have come to the Temple in the years since it opened, many just to sit and meditate, to absorb its beautiful atmosphere, and then to go back to their own path, their own work, with renewed inspiration. So the Temple has also become a meeting place between workers and seekers of many paths, as well as between the two worlds of earth and spirit.

'It is almost impossible to define the inspiration which has come to so many White Eagle workers, members and friends all over the world as a direct result of the Temple being here in visible form. It is indeed as though heaven and earth meet here. When one is in the Temple, either in the physical body or in meditation, it is easy to draw aside the veil and touch the heaven world, and to realise the oneness of all life. It is our centre, the receptacle for the inspiration and healing which radiates to workers all over the world. Each group, each individual member, is linked in spirit with the Star and thus with the Temple (which is the physical counterpart of the Star Temple in spirit), and through this link each is strengthened in his own work of radiating the Light of spiritual healing into the world. Many who have never seen the Temple find they can come in thought and be part of the work, and share in the peace and blessing which flows from it. A typical letter came to us from a new member in Nigeria: "Thank you for the 'Light' from the White Temple. Its radiance is reaching me and my people here and we are being healed all round". Visiting members, seeing the Temple for the first time, so often feel at home, as though they have been here many times before; and a poem which was contributed to STELLA POLARIS perhaps sums up the power which the Temple has on the imagination:

A view along the front of the Temple extension shortly after completion

> '… I looked back at the Temple as I left,
> but did not leave.
> For now the Light illumines
> all I see and think and understand.
> We are all stars,
> made bright with love,
> and when I think of it,
> I want to dance.
> *Enid McGilvray, in* STELLA POLARIS, *August-September 1984*

'More and more as we take the services we are aware of a Lodge in the world of spirit "similar to our Temple building on earth, yet much more beautiful and harmonious, where the work continues in an unbroken stream"
(*Joan Hodgson in* STELLA POLARIS, *August-September 1984).*

'We are aware constantly of White Eagle's presence, and of Minesta's and Brother Faithful's: not only as we go about our own work but through the letters we receive from members and friends all over the world. Not least from absent healing patients, who write of remarkable experiences when White Eagle, or Minesta or Brother Faithful, has made themselves known to them; or how, through extraordinary 'coincidence', a loving White Eagle helper was brought to them at a time of need. The knowledge that White Eagle is with us was confirmed for us recently in a very evidential way when the autobiography appeared of the medium Ursula Roberts. Writing of how she is conscious not only of her own spirit guide but of

THE TEMPOL OF GO D isx a plas
weree pepol wereshi p . i t is xixx xxx
a house of god, he livsse xixxxx there
be kosse Itixxx it is kviut and
pisc) foll   xixxxxt the end

Young reader's contribution to
STELLA POLARIS

A view along the front of the New Lands office extension shortly after completion

others – such as Silver Birch – she told how (to her) White Eagle frequently appeared

in a great hazy light in the centre of which was a form reminiscent of an Indian chieftain. I have seen this vision when with people about whom nothing is known to me and I invariably take it as a sign that such people are associated with the White Eagle teachings; this is always confirmed by them and accepted as a gratifying indication that this loving spirit is aware of the thoughts of the people who read the transcripts of his teachings as given through his medium.

Ursula Roberts, LIVING IN TWO WORLDS

'So White Eagle fulfils a promise that he made to us as the phase of his communication through Minesta closed: that we would never be without him, or his guidance and love. And this is indeed true. Many, we repeat, when going through a time of great stress, have felt his brotherly strength and encouragement, lifting or comforting them, helping them to see the Christ Light. We feel him raising for us, gradually, the veil on the future, showing us the way forward, helping us to avoid mistakes, pointing to opportunities, giving us the vision we need.'

THE STORY OF THE WHITE EAGLE LODGE

BROTHERS THROUGH THE YEARS

On these two pages, the photographs are chosen almost at random out of our archives. They stand for a huge number, over our seventy-five years, whom it is impossible to represent here. For a key to these pages, see p. 159.

CHAPTER VI

On up the Mountain

THE CELEBRATION of the Lodge's fiftieth birthday in 1986 started in March, and appropriately in London. 'We don't think the London Lodge has ever seen anything like it', Colum exclaimed in his report in STELLA POLARIS, after almost every item of furniture was removed from the main chapel to accommodate eager attenders at a full week of events of different kinds. The furniture removal (and oh! how many times has the London Lodge furniture been moved round for an event!) was no mean feat; but it was felt that the resultant pulled muscles were worth it. There was a real sense of ushering in the next fifty years through a fiesta of music, flowers and lovingly-prepared food, and the climax was a moving spiritual communion that celebrated the first fifty years of a spiritual philosophy that had already helped so many. Brothers re-dedicated themselves to the spiritual work of healing and sending out the light, and the presence of the angels and brothers in spirit was felt to be almost palpable. A true celebration.

Ylana, Joan and John stand under White Eagle's picture at the members' party for the Golden Jubilee in London in March 1986

It did not stop with the end of that week…. The celebrations continued throughout the year, one of renewed spiritual purpose and joyful service, and it reached a peak in June at New Lands. One key event was an extra-special Garden Party on the lawn. 1986 was the first year that a marquee was put up in New Lands garden, entertaining the office staff (or distracting them?) as clashing poles and creaking canvas interrupted their usually idyllic view of the wooded glades of Monk's walk. On the day, many prayers of thanks were said for that creaking canvas, when the rain poured down all afternoon … although our thanks to the weather spirits were perhaps a little less fervent! It was noted that people really appreciated the marquee and it became a fixture for future years, having thoroughly proved its worth.

Yet possibly the highlight of the year was the grand Jubilee Concert, held in the Temple on Saturday 14 June, the culmination of the extraordinary work and effort made by the choir of all ages, led by choirmaster Simon Bentley and accompanied by organist Philip Jones, who also provided solo items. Simon certainly outdid himself in 1986, schooling his choir to produce stirring and ambitious music to a professional standard; their programme stretched from Bach

Philip at the Temple organ, before a Sunday service

The Golden Jubilee Concert choir, with Simon (centre) and soloists Sylvia Morton and Timothy Sutton

Simon Bentley today

to Britten. Our photograph shows how Simon also held the choir to a rigorous – and glamorous – dress code, a visual surprise for an audience used to a gallery of simple white robes!

Another rich memory of that day is the evening party held in the Meeting Room and under canvas outside it. It was a blissfully lovely June day, and the evening sunshine illuminated everyone as they strolled with friends and half-empty glasses across Temple hill or sat gazing into the west.

Both Philip and Simon demonstrate how rich in talent the Lodge had become by the mid-1980s. Philip first came to us in London (one of many whose first introduction to the Lodge was reading the words of Lord Dowding in his books MANY MANSIONS and LYCHGATE) in the 1950s, and with the wonderful credentials of having been sub-organist at the Church of St Bartholomew the Great, Smithfield. Living in Ruislip, he and his dear wife Olive met and brought to the Lodge in 1960 Jim and Norah Ackroyd, who remained stalwarts of the London Lodge until their passing in 2007. Soon Philip was taking his place as organist in the London Lodge alongside Mary Brameld; and after the opening of the Temple in 1974 he must have spent hours and hours in transit between the two Mother Lodges to play the organ first at one and then at the other. He was above all a sensitive soloist and only ceased regular playing in the Temple a few years ago in his late eighties. He has now (as we write) attained the remarkable age of 94 and has just given up driving himself a mile and a half to the Temple, though he comes when given a lift.

Simon, though a talented musician, came more through the

GOLDEN JUBILEE PARTY AND AVEBURY—NEW LANDS WALK

Opposite page: Participants in the sunshine at the Golden Jubilee party in June 1986 (top left and right). Middle, the walkers set off from Avebury to New Lands with (below) some scenes from the walk. Above (this page) the Star marker chalked on gateposts did us proud if routefinding was hard.

Astrology School, having been shown Joan's articles in STELLA POLARIS while a student at Trinity College, Cambridge. Asked, he will tell a remarkable story of how these articles, offered by fellow-student Colum Hayward, miraculously found their way through a locked door into his room! Before he came into the Lodge full-time (as he did in 1985), Simon acquired most useful horticultural experience at the RHS garden near Wisley in Surrey. Coming into the Lodge, he was able to act as Joan's next-in-command in the Astrology School and to bring professionalism to the running of the New Lands estate – as well as run the Choir!

Back to 1986. Early in October, and as already reported, twenty-six brave walkers set off on their eighty-mile, four-day 'Jubilee pilgrimage': walking from the ancient spiritual site of Avebury in Wiltshire to New Lands. Seen also as a pilgrimage for peace, the walk was a symbolic journey, allowing the twenty-six to make their own pledge of service for the years ahead but also providing an opportunity for fun and friendship (there's nothing like working together against adversity for really cementing a friendship!) among the walkers who took part. The walk was organised and led by Michael Sage, a seemingly indefatigable, fit and endlessly patient leader, who calmly allowed those less steady to follow in his firm footsteps … and a true sense of Brotherhood was induced out of the various mishaps that occurred, including enlisting a friendly farmer to tow one of the support cars out of a rutted and muddy lane, under cover of darkness! The walk, Colum observed in STELLA POLARIS, could be seen as a symbol of our progress on the spiritual path – although one might hope that less emphasis would be placed in the next world on muddy wellies!

Jubilee year was a genuinely unforgettable time in the Lodge, and notable in many ways. It stands out as the year that a computer was first introduced to New Lands – what a momentous day, in retrospect! – enabling Betty Barber, the redoubtable records officer (not to mention fundraising stamp-collector extraordinare) to begin entering approximately seven thousand names and addresses on the temperamental new database (yet another test of stamina and endurance that year!). 1986 was also the year in which it became obvious that the White Eagle work had genuinely 'gone global', as the Jubilee celebrations were shared by the worldwide family of White Eagle and 'Letters, cards and flowers brought much love from groups and individuals around the world' (STELLA POLARIS). It was becoming clear that the distance between Brothers was really unimportant, with all being together, united in spirit. This love from around the world, and these sense of reduced separateness, has truly formed the keynote for the years that have followed it.

*

The centre pages of STELLA POLARIS tell us in 1986 that 'the emphasis in our Golden Year is on expansion overseas…. We are standing on the threshold of a new era'. Prophetic words! The fast, far-reaching expansion of the White Eagle work all over the world in the 1980s and since has been an inspiring process. For instance, at the end of 1987, White Eagle's teachings were in print in fourteen different languages. Rapid change was taking place at exhilarating speed in at least three continents.

In Australia, the White Eagle work had been led for many years by Doris and Alf Commins, who had established a White Eagle centre in the hills at Maleny, Queensland, in 1982. Doris and Alf were ably supported in their hard work by daughters Lyn and Gay. In 1986, their spiritual work had already expanded significantly; a report at the time tells us that 'the little wooden chapel was filled to bursting'. It was clear that the time was right to expand physically too. Retreats were already held regularly in such accommodation as there was at the centre, but it was perfectly clear that it could not function properly until a more substantial place of worship was built..

That same year, Jenny visited America to report on the land north of Houston, Texas, that had been purchased for a new retreat centre there by Jean LeFevre, the leader of the work in the Americas. Jean's example as a White Eagle worker is outstanding. She had began her tireless work for the light while still in Britain, founding what was originally just the Crowborough Daughter Lodge in 1975; in the next decade, her work led her to the United States to found and develop a new Americas centre there with the support of her husband John. The acquisition of the land, on the edge of the township of Montgomery, was the first stage, and this is what Jenny went to see. She loved the new location, describing it as 'quite magical, with a feeling of White Eagle's presence already. There is even a double circle of tall pines creating a natural temple. The land drops gently to a most attractive lake and there are many trees and flowering shrubs…. The plan is to put a ready-built wooden house on the site so that retreats can start very soon'.

Very soon indeed. The hardworking American brothers had services going before the end of the year, despite the fact that, as Colum put it in STELLA POLARIS, 'the only commodity which is in strong supply is faith!' These services took place in the little Rose Chapel, sadly no longer standing. One who was present then writes today: 'I remember the Rose Chapel very well. The first service was actually held at Christmas in 1986. The final papers had not been signed officially, but the first service was in that wonderful place. Brother Lawrence suspended a torch to bring some light, before the electricity was installed. I may not be the best person to describe the chapel as I didn't live locally, although of course I visited many times. The chairs were what we call 'ice-cream parlor' chairs, and were covered and nailed into place by wonderful volunteers. A soft pink cover

Gay and Lyn Commins, as they then were, when we first knew them

THE STORY OF THE WHITE EAGLE LODGE

The Rose Chapel in the pines in Texas

was used, with white metal scrolled backs. About eighteen could fit inside the chapel: the regular congregation was about nine, sometimes more, at that time [so was it in New Lands chapel, in the early days!]. We so loved our little Rose Chapel in the pines … the path leading to it was lined with crystals which sparkled in the moonlight – magical to say the least!'

Vision and tireless leadership were not confined to Australia and America. Expansion in Europe was also in the cards for 1987. A new Swedish centre was opened, in peaceful countryside near Gothenburg. Another description of beautiful land is coming! 'The ground around the house is terraced and there are some lovely old trees.… We have seen many elks, and some of them have eaten the buds from the rhododendrons!' The isolated site is ten miles from the nearest village, providing visitors with a wonderful experience of the rural beauty of Sweden.

An early work party there

This beauty was much appreciated by Jenny and Geoffrey Dent, when they took their family on a visit to Sweden the following year. Geoffrey wrote: 'The Minesta Retreat and Healing Centre … is surrounded by pine trees and still lakes. This lovely situation, deep in the heart of nature, seemed to make for us an especially strong link with the North American Indians and bring the personality of

White Eagle very close…. Sandor and his wife Sirkka opened the centre and have created a truly beautiful sanctuary, both on the outer and the inner planes.' Thirteen people attended Jenny and Geoffrey's retreat, which 'included morning meditations, evening talks and walks in the countryside'. 'One of our special memories', Geoffrey continued, 'is of the meals, mostly prepared from food grown organically at the centre'. The Dent family also recalled 'the most succulent wild mushrooms, picked that morning from the ancient pinewoods surrounding the centre, and sautéed in butter'. Clear evidence, not for the first time, that a successful retreat also requires a satisfied stomach!

The Sandor mentioned by Geoffrey is Sandor Huszár, who had taken over leadership of the work in Sweden from the pioneering Aina Kinde, who deserves a few words here. Called by White Eagle 'Silver Star of Sweden', Aina was our pioneer brother in this country, and started our first group there. She later met Sandor, who was already well-known in Swedish spiritual circles as a healer, and – loving White Eagle deeply – he started to work with her, so that in due course she handed on the torch to him. The subsequent progress of the work in Sweden was such that Geoffrey returned there in 1992, with Joan Hodgson, to perform the inauguration ceremony for the new Swedish Daughter Lodge, a ceremony that celebrated and emphasised the importance of the work in Sweden to White Eagle's worldwide family, and the wisdom, dedication and commitment of Sandor and his hardworking and supportive family. Sandor described the centre and the members who are so committed to its work:' Members came from all over Sweden to help us…. We now have meditations and retreats, and people come for the peace, and they love walking through the forests and hearing the natural sounds. There are no cars, all is still, and we feel the angels close'.

Like many other overseas leaders, Sandor was also closely engaged in the translation of the White Eagle books: 'We have eighteen White Eagle books published in Swedish. THE ILLUMINED ONES has sold 2,500 copies and we are using the royalties to print a book in Hungarian about the White Eagle work … so the work will grow there in the future, too!' (It has!)

Hard work in Sweden: Sandor Huszár and his son Michel construct the basement offices below the new building

*

Further important developments were taking place on the other side of the world. The Commins family received plans for the building of the new Temple, and in 1988 Doris and Lyn headed to England to discuss them with the Lodge Mothers, Joan and Ylana. To the excitement of all, guidance was received during their visit to proceed with the plans. Doris Commins later wrote: 'Work on clearing the land will begin almost immediately, and then the foundations will –

Doris Commins

Work begins on the Australasian Temple; the lone figure on the concrete slabs is Doris Commins

in the material and the spiritual sense – be dug…. The whole centre will be finished in white just like our Temple at New Lands…. The lands at Willomee form the crown of a valley, which is green along its ridge and falls off into the untouched rain forest. The new building looks down into the valley, whose arms reach out either side in a gentle embrace of nature. A wonderful spot'. The new Temple was planned to seat 200 in the main chapel and include five small chapels, a library and a large meeting room. The next stage of the plan would include a retreat centre to sleep ten, possessing a magnificent view over the valley. Doris added that 'the whole concept is to have a place of beauty, where the surroundings reflect the beauty within each and every one of us'.

What an extraordinary time of development and progress! The two continents of Australasia and America seemed to pace each other as they developed their beautiful temples and centres. In July 1989 Colum visited America to visit the burdgeoning groups across North America and to lead a retreat with Jean LeFevre; he wrote of his 'deep admiration of the work done by Jean, and by John and their wonderful team'. In all, he visited groups in New York, Connecticut, Texas, Los Angeles, Minneosota and Toronto.

Just how impressive this work was became clear when the plans for the new American retreat centre were unveiled later that year. The retreat centre, designed to sleep twenty, included a central meeting room for community study during retreats. Further up the hill, the site for the Temple – expected to follow in due course – was described as 'a place of inner beauty and mystery … one ascends along the pathway through the woods – along which, we feel sure, the ancient brethren have walked and indeed still walk'.

In 1990, STELLA POLARIS published a plan of the land at the new American centre, together with this evocative description: 'Come for a walk with us round the Retreat Centre land in Texas … a happy stroll down the hill to the creek, passing on the way a blue

New York W. E. Group in 1989

French retreat outside Paris at Plailly, June 1991

THE STORY OF THE WHITE EAGLE LODGE

haze of Texan bluebells at the right time of the year.... Come back up the hill to follow the thin corridor in the wood to a finger of land on the true crest of the hill. This is where the eventual Temple for the Americas will stand, some time in the not too distant future. Meditate here as you wish, and then follow the shaded path through to the lake, whose little island adds grace to the setting. Across a paddock of land as you continue, there stands at last the site for the new Retreat Home.... Can you help us create this dream?' Those words remind us that as in previous appeals in which seemingly Herculean tasks were accomplished, the huge achievements of the centres overseas were made possible by the fundraising, generosity and sheer hard work of White Eagle's worldwide family. Credit also lay with the exceptionally committed and talented workers within the centres themselves, all giving support that was practical, financial, spiritual ... and effective.

Native Aerican reminders at the Texas center. The flower is the Indian Paintbrush

Sometimes the talent came not only from the workers and leaders whose names are 'writ large' already in this book. If we take on case, Brother Lawrence at the Texas Center, he may in his simple generosity stand for many. His introduction to the Lodge was an unusual one. At one stage of his life a Benedictine monk, he was so outraged by proposals in the US to overturn native American land rights and mine uranium on tribal lands, that with a very few companions he set off for a much-publicised walk across America as part of the campaign against the mining. Shortly before he left, he came upon the little book PRAYER IN THE NEW AGE and had it with him throughout, using it every day. It was, he said, the only thing at the time that enabled him to make sense of life. The walk over, he visited us in London, spent time at Mary Hershey's group in Long Beach, California (see the photograph on p. 91; Lawrence is shown in Texas on p. 97), and finally devoted himself totally to Jean's work at St John's Retreat Center at Montgomery .

At the Center there his monastic talents came to the fore: the name 'Lawrence' was his own choice and he indeed saw God in the pots and pans ... and put God into the food he cooked. He saw God, too, in the mowing machines and the garden tools and the book despatch materials; but he also approached the rituals of the Lodge with the deepest understanding and sincerity. He knew too that everyone, regardless of orientation, colour, oddness of behaviour is welcome in White Eagle's home so long as their behaviours do not make its peace unavailable to others; and Lawrence stands as a symbol of *inclusion* in the Lodge – particularly in the case of sexual orientation.

In 1990 the Australian Temple was moving fast towards completion and Doris Commins wrote, 'We had some landscapers in and one who was particularly interested said, "Oh, there is a presence here already". And when he entered the Temple, under the dome he just stood in awe looking up'. Then followed a series of 'mini-miracles' that enabled the work to finish on time. For instance, the altar arrived 'weighing 400 kilos – that is nearly as heavy as six men! Rather more than six men puzzled just that question, with increasing concern. Then the miracle! A large truck appeared in the driveway, two weeks behind schedule with his load of wooden planks for garden paths. On the truck's back, a crane!' Another miracle was the presence of Mary Hershey, visiting from the Los Angeles Daughter Lodge, who played the organ at the opening when no-one else was available.

This type of practical support – so typical of the Lodge and yet so unexpected until it happens – was invaluable, right up to the opening service, with 'all sorts of stories of people rallying round to help. The officiants' chairs and reading desks were finished on the morning of the opening service, thanks to emergency work by volunteers and the local upholsterer. The winged disc was set up over the entrance by the willing member who had made it, John Corbett, the same morning. The landscaped slopes in front of the Temple were planted out just a few days earlier' But despite the last-minute activity, 'the service, when it came, brought peace, and all the mad preparations were forgotten. Within days, people were feeling that the Temple had been there for years and years'

The Temple was opened in September before a congregation of 230, by Ylana Hayward, with Doris at her side. So great was the support that a further Thanksgiving Service had to be held the next week, with 200 people present this time. Ylana stayed to lead other activities, including two meditation classes with over 100 participants.

Australasian Temple opening

to the work by becoming Brothers, or by joining in the healing work as absent and contact healers. It was and is a true testament to the strong heart of the White Eagle purpose, and one that heralded a period of change and development in the healing work.

Opening of the Leeds Lodge: Joan and John with Bettine Pickles, who truly pioneered the way for something that has been a most successful story ever since

Outward pressures as well as our own needs indicated that the time had come to develop new and more formal standards in the training of contact healers, and also for there to be a code of conduct agreed across the main healing organisations which would be a basis of seeking the trust of the medical profession. This work was pioneered by a new national umbrella group, the Confederation of Healing Organisations (CHO), which worked to raise public trust and respect for healing, not only with the medical establishment but also at a political level. Jeremy Hayward, now in charge of the healing, explained that there had been 'a growing, collective awareness among different spiritual healing organisations that we needed to join together'. Working on behalf of our growing band of healers representatives from the Lodge took part in due course in a ground breaking experiment of developing an National Vocational Qualification (NVQ)-style qualification for healers, which of course involved enormously greater formality in assessment. Although changes in the wider political landscape prevented the full introduction of this, the qualification the work involved brought real gain for the healing organisations involved. And we are proud to claim that while standards are better, the true White Eagle healing remains at heart exactly the same.

At the level of human hospitality, the London Lodge has been pleased to host CHO's council meetings over many years, alongside a number of similar meetings.

The design of White Eagle books has developed over the years. In the case of WISDOM IN THE STARS, *there was a new cover in 1959 shown left, a colour one in 1973 (middle) and another in 1991 (right). Astrological teaching began in the 1940s; we note a meeting of the 'Astrological Lodge' in December 1949*

The growing demand for the White Eagle message at this time also led to developments within the Publishing Trust. 1988 saw a publishing milestone, with the millionth White Eagle book being sold. The first books, A LITTLE BOOK OF PRAYERS and ILLUMINATION, were published in 1937, and the sale of the millionth book, notionally a copy of SPIRITUAL UNFOLDMENT 3, was announced at the Lodge's fifty-second anniversary party in the London Lodge. The symbolism of the million books was particularly important, as the publications remain the main way in which White Eagle's philosophy can first reach those in need. Their continued publication highlighted the spread of the light across the world, a network of light spread by each book and each reader, each in turn passing their illumination on in service to others.

Pausing in our main narrative, let us just stop to consider all those involved in producing the White Eagle books over the years, since their success is so much at the heart of the whole work. There are firstly those who 'took down' White Eagle's talks: Ylana Hayward from the beginning, then Sara Burdett, Serena Bumford, and many others. Brother Faithful not only edited virtually all the books up to around 1950 (training Ylana to follow him – she was certainly involved in the 1949 LIVING WORD and the 1955 MEDITATION), he also had a huge influence on their design and on the employment of the artists who decorated them in the 1940s. (Joan Hodgson was writing about astrology and health from the 1940s on, but we are currently noting not authors but the unsung heroes – the editors, and their redoubtable proofreaders, with Alison Innes queen among those!). In the early 1950s Geoffrey Hayward started to make his huge contribution, too – something we have already commented on, as we have with the most successful White Eagle book ever, THE QUIET MIND, which was compiled by Ylana. While at university in the early 1970s, their sons Colum and Jeremy started to make a contribution, and each has now many compilations of teaching behind them. Colum steered the Publishing Trust through a programme of re-editing the books in the 1980s and 1990s: much misunderstood, this programme was principally designed to improve the text by comparison with the original scripts. Now, in the twenty-first century, another Hayward, Anna, has joined the editorial team, while Sara Cody, too, has initiated more than one new book, including the first draft of this one in its revised form.

But to return to 1988. The general expansion led to the employment of Nigel Millross from that autumn. He had come into the London Lodge first in 1980 at the age of 16, one of its youngest-ever new recruits and active in our Young People's Group after. Working alongside Colum in London, Nigel left his mark by designing many covers for White Eagle books, as well as the very first White Eagle Lodge website (at the end of the 1990s), many of the beautiful features of which are still to be seen today. In the 1990s, he was also responsible for the design and make-up of STELLA POLARIS, and he still works on the astrology journal ALTAIR. He also worked throughout its publication on a little French version of STELLA POLARIS, developed and edited by Monique Regester, and called LES FEUILLETS D'AIGLE BLANC.

Joan Hodgson led the anniversary service that year (1988), giving 'a wonderful vision of the ever-unfolding future of the work' which was reflected in the stirring hymn, 'These things shall be', described at the time as 'extraordinarily fitting' and always a hymn guaranteed to raise the rafters, 'with its vision of the other world and of the New Age'. STELLA POLARIS reported that 'The veil seemed very thin, and White Eagle very close to us all'.

The thin veil between this world and the world of spirit was especially and even painfully to be noticed at this time, with the passing of many much-loved members of White Eagle's family into the world of light. First to leave us were Joan Punchard and Alison Innes, both in 1987, after quite a period of illness in each case. Joan stands alongside Teddy Dent at the head of our rank of White

In 1990 the Publishing Trust launched its first yoga book, YOGA OF THE HEART *by Jenny Beeken (pictured, with Geoffrey Dent)*

Eagle poets. She had also been librarian of the London Lodge after 'Peace' Brown, and her name here stands actually for a little group of four immensely loved brothers in London, the others being Rhona Philips, Mary Sears and Dorrie Lyon (Dorrie outlived them all, passing years later, in 2004 at the age of 97!). Alison, later known by her Brotherhood name, Pearl, had been at the heart of the work for 44 years and has already received much mention: she was mourned not least by the generation of grown-up White Eagle children whom she had 'baby-sat' constantly: Rose, Jenny, Colum and Jeremy. We miss her services as we write, as proofreader without parallel.

Alison doing what she so much loved: looking after the 'children' in the 1950s

Irene Hancock, better known in the Lodge by the name White Eagle gave her, Radiance, left her physical body in May 1989, in South Devon, where she had spent her last few weeks with her family. Radiance has been mentioned earlier in this book in connection with her many years of service as a leader of the London Lodge, but from 1979 she lived in 'Sun Cottage' on the New Lands estate, and on top of many more outwardly significant duties was arranging flowers, consummately, almost to the end. Above all, her immensely deep wisdom was appreciated in her role as a Trustee of the Lodge. Once, she had been Personal Private Secretary to Prime Minister Stanley Baldwin, so the intricacies of legislation and authority were easy for her. She had a nice contempt for red tape! Childless herself, she was probably godmother to more White Eagle children than anyone in history, whether officially or by later adoption. 'Auntie Re' as the Hodgson and Hayward children knew her, was loved by them all; in the next generation, Sara Dent (Cody) and Michael Dent saw her as an 'honorary aunt' who prepared lovely teas. Sara remembers playing traditional games of dominoes in her cosy sitting room.

Radiance, on a vvisit with Minesta and Brother Faithful to see Burstow again (1960)

Radiance often acted as 'Mother' for the New Lands retreats, as well as performing endless invaluable duties around the estate. Ylana Hayward, perhaps her closest friend, wrote at the time of her passing: 'I cannot remember when Radiance first took on the task of making the Lodge beautiful with flowers … she gave so much to us all of sheer beauty and inspiration through those flower arrangements…. I think her love in those tasks brought the angels very close.' Radiance was, in Ylana's words 'a woman whose whole life had been devoted to giving and serving and doing…. I shall always remember her as I sat by her side in our Inner Brotherhood work, being so aware of how utterly still and clear her mind was as she did the work, a perfect tool for her shining spirit.' Dear Radiance: it was in many ways you that saw the Rose Star symbol drawn and brought into our work: it is a symbol of your life, too, the rose blooming upon the star. Her co-Trustee for many years, Noel Gabriel, passed in 1994 and has been mentioned before; few better than he brought a sense of the inner mystery, or mysteries, of the work.

THE STORY OF THE WHITE EAGLE LODGE

Noel and Loveday Gabriel, photographed in 1974

And the other especially shining spirit was John Hodgson, who passed soon after: the man whom many had regarded as the 'Father' of the Lodge work since Brother Faithful's passing. Much has been written of him already, but his very sudden and unexpected release into the world of light in January 1990 was a wonderful moment for his soul – so many people felt conscious of the angelic welcome he received – but it was an enormous shock for those left behind that such a hale and hearty man had been taken from his physical body so quickly. (John, of Yorkshire farming stock and a 'Yorkshire-man' in the full sense of the word, would never wear more than a token scarf around his neck, even on the coldest day, as he strode around New Lands estate, keeping a fatherly eye on goings on). At his funeral, Geoffrey's Dent's words that John's passing had been 'dead easy' were so characteristically 'John' that we knew he had said them himself, in his soft Yorkshire and with a twinkle in his eye. Many Members' Parties had been spiced up by John's wit, and his extraordinary repertoire of stories from the past.

When John passed, Joan – his wife of forty-seven years – lived the truth of the White Eagle teaching quite literally. With faith so strong, it was almost tangible; she provided a shining support for her family, healing her own grief in the light of the Star and through her ongoing contact with John in spirit. She was herself an amazing example of the reality of the healing power that she and John, as joint Healing Secretaries, had helped so many to receive. Nevertheless, the physical presence of John was much missed (and continues to be missed.) He was *such* an extra-special man, and one who brought enormous humour into the work. STELLA POLARIS reported that not many people knew 'how completely his attendance to her practical needs made possible the continuation of Minesta's work, just as he managed, guarded and cherished the work of his wife Joan.' Essentially a practical man, whose views echoed White Eagle's teaching on the need to 'scrub the floor of your Lodge', John was himself an example to others of how to remain with your feet on the ground in a spiritual setting. A visitor to the Temple recalled their amusement when a visiting group were asked to remove their shoes on entering the building. An earnest individual was surprisingly keen to comply. 'Walking barefoot must allow the spiritual vibrations to enter the soles of your feet!', he exclaimed excitedly, to John's slight amusement. 'No', John replied dryly, 'We don't want a lot of dirt on the carpet.'

John worked as Treasurer of the Lodge for many years, and Ylana wrote that his 'steady guiding hand and great faith helped to steer the Lodge through those difficult early years when we never quite knew where the next penny was coming from.' He was also well known and loved by many for his work as Healing Secretary. A deeply kind man with tremendous human sympathies, he cheered so many healing patients with his little notes and cards, all signed with his characteristic squiggle of a happy little person. He was an entertaining and idiosyncratic raconteur, and his stories enlivened many a service or event. After his death, Ylana wrote: 'I feel that any words of mine are totally inadequate to pay just tribute' to John, and quoted from some of the letters received at New Lands when people heard the news, including this one, which ran:

John at the Golden Jubilee celebrations in 1986

'His lovely sense of humour was such a joy, and stopped us getting too serious.… John's love of his family, and the way in which he protected and cherished you, is a lasting example to us all. We feel thankful and privileged to have known him.

A particularly lovely confirmation of John's contact with his family after death was described by his daughter Jenny, in February 1990. John had been excitedly looking forward to the birth of his second great-grandchild, to Kate (Rose's eldest daughter) and Gordon, especially as the baby was due on his birthday. Jenny wrote: 'Two days before what would have been my father's birthday, I was suddenly aware of him, looking so young and happy, holding a lovely little baby.… He was beaming all over his face and said very clearly 'Here's my birthday girl!'. Then, when 3 February came, I was thinking rather sadly, 'Oh, I must have been wrong, we'd have heard something by now if the baby were coming today'. Almost immediately, there was my father again, as clear as if he were physically in the room. He was again holding the baby and I heard him say, so clearly, 'The baby's coming at 7 o'clock!' I thought I was getting carried away by my imagination. However, at 8 pm the phone went and the news was that Jessica Louise had been born to Kate at 7.03 pm'. This wonderful confirmation was later explained by Jenny as particularly appropriate: 'Using time to convey a proof to me is exactly what he would do, because we were both alike in being over-anxious about time and particularly arriving on time!'

More news for the family at New Lands came a year after John's passing, when Jeremy Hayward and Anna Dacre were married in the Temple. Their wedding was a day blessed with sunshine after a long period of dark skies and icy wind and rain. 'What a lovely gift from God to start the day', a guest commented. The reception was held in the Temple meeting room, and we remember that it included a gourmet meal ending with a featherlight Baked Alaska – quite an achievement for the caterers who were bringing all the cooked dishes some distance from the kitchen at New Lands house. Anna soon proved herself a multitalented and valuable addition to the family. Being a trained counsellor, yoga teacher and talented writer, not to mention artist, she was soon showing enormous creativity in her ongoing work in the Lodge.

Anna and Jeremy, singing along at a Garden Party

*

THE STORY OF THE WHITE EAGLE LODGE

1992 came to be thought of as the Lodge's *annus mirablis* because 'so many wonderful things happened' and in so many different countries. Fittingly, this was also an important anniversary year. One hundred years after the birth of Grace Cooke, the time had come to appreciate her efforts and her legacy – that of the White Eagle work itself. MINESTA'S VISION, the centenary collection of her writings, was published to celebrate her achievements, and the year became one long round of special birthday 'presents' in her memory, from different corners of the globe.

To recount those we begin in London, where in a sense the celebrations began a year early. Minesta's centenary came swiftly after the London Lodge's Golden Jubilee in 1991, at which the 'Golden Mountain Appeal' for a 'new' London Lodge had been launched. In many ways, the launching of the appeal was seen as the start of Minesta's centenary celebrations, a particularly appropriate tribute. Among the things that were most admirable in Minesta were her determination and her ability to succeed despite all material odds. Her strength of purpose was described movingly in STELLA POLARIS: 'For her, the service of the spirit was all-important … once she was certain that spirit required a course of action, then she was quite unshakeable in her purpose. She would move against all earthly advice to achieve what they asked. And the Lodge is her memorial.'

The London Lodge building as we know it had been commenced just before the First World War. Amusingly, when it was first seen as a replacement for Pembroke Hall, Minesta had remembered pushing Joan, in the pram, past it while it was under construction. Most of it dates from 1913, and that was the year Joan was born, at the end of July. Today's roof pattern shows how many times the building was extended, all of them apparently in a very short space of time. Evidently the School of Animal Painting had been a dramatic success. To our misfortune, those extensions seem to have been added altogether too fast, and that shows not only in the standard of building, but also in the design of the whole: a very large proportion of the roof drains into the middle and rainwater flows out through the building itself, creating a huge danger of flooding for both upstairs and down. Those who work there have lost count of the number of times this has happened. And decorations suffered each time. Another flood sometimes came up from below, when the street drain blocked. The heating system was overdue for replacement, and rewiring required by law.

Also, space was short. A new meditative service upstairs in the Brotherhood Chapel had proved so popular the room would no longer always hold the people who came. We felt the pinch in healing services too, and there was a general feeling of falling over ourselves all through the week. STELLA POLARIS reported at the time that 'The London Lodge has seen fifty years of service. The atmosphere

Our veritable 'Golden Mountain', which led the appeal in the London Lodge

that has been built up there will go on … far into the future…. But the material shell will not.'

Three courses of action seemed possible. One was refurbishment, but that did not solve the roofing issue. Another was the same plus a new roof. The latter would be enormously expensive because the poorly-dovetailing extensions of the building would all need to come under one canopy draining outwards, and party walls gave no scope for external drainage except towards the front – which meant largely into the courtyard. The rebuilding of the London Lodge was, of the three, the most attractive, because it solved all the problems and might create a landmark building that would bring worldwide attention to the work – but at what cost! At the time it seemed most certainly a course of action required by spirit, and it was Joan above all who held the vision of a new building altogether, and who launched the Golden Mountain Appeal. She was in many ways as courageous as her mother, Minesta, when it came to big challenges.

The London Brothers chose to see it rather as an opportunity than as a dire challenge: 'We have the choice of re-creating it in any way that we wish. Our material reconstruction is also our spiritual recreation, the shedding of an old coat and emergence as a new and more beautiful being for the next stage of our work'. The symbol of the Golden Mountain was decided upon for the Appeal because 'that mountain is one we all walk up and at times climb somewhat laboriously. But when we remember the spirit world, and the love that surrounds all life, it becomes a mountain not of drear rock but of pure gold…. Let us keep our vision on the summit of the mountain'. A model mountain was set up in the London Lodge, steadily becoming more gold as it filled with pound coins, and a major fundraising initiative was launched to celebrate the Golden Jubilee and Minesta's centenary. Within a few months the total had reached £5000 and we were off on our way, up the foothills of that mountain.

This growth of the fund continued to accelerate in 1992 through the efforts of Lodge members and friends. The list of small fundraising activities was almost endless, from quiz nights to recycled cards but the ideas, large and small, went on and on and the money poured in to that mountain. Among larger events, one of the most memorable fundraisers was the 87-mile sponsored 'Super-walk' along the South Downs. Walkers started off near Eastbourne and spent several days walking back to New Lands, accompanied on the final leg by coachloads more joining in the annual one-day sponsored walk, which by then had become an annual event.

The walk was described as a triumph of brotherhood over adversity (in the form of the mixed weather conditions – the final miles of the walk being completed in driving rain!). The group bonded 'despite its great diversity. Between the oldest of the party and the youngest, [there was] a gap of fifty-three years, and yet a happy and growing

The old Lodge: all decked out for Christmas, and the Brotherhood Chapel

Tea stop on one of our many sponsored walks

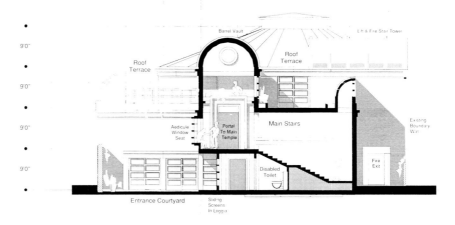

sense of group identity all the time.' The walk gained over £8,000 towards climbing the foothills of the Golden Mountain appeal.

The actual centenary of Minesta's birth was celebrated with a special Hundredth 'Birthday Present' – the architect's plans for the new London Lodge. They were presented with appropriate ceremony on Sunday 7 June (her actual centenary fell two days later). The main chapel in the London Lodge was filled with a sense of expectancy, blackened-out windows adding an air of mystery and excitement which was increased when the choir began to sing the Hallelujah chorus from Handel's *Messiah* – stirring music for an important occasion in the London Lodge's history. Mark Leslie, the architect, was the son of an old member of the Lodge, Desmond Leslie. When Mark displayed his design for the new London Lodge, and when it was projected in the main chapel there was 'an audible gasp'. Mark had created a design with 'an air of mystery to it; a hint of the past, and a feeling of a completely new age to come'. Colum wrote at the time 'There is a great sense of ceremonial to it. But the challenge … was to preserve this scheme while making it gentle, creating, to use our favourite phrase, a "simple home of love"'. STELLA POLARIS reported: 'We hope … that you will feel it is a fitting birthday present to our beloved Mother, Minesta, and that it honours the divine in all of us, the home of the spirit'.

From the outset, it was a rewarding example of the power of the spirit and of faith that the money raised at each stage of the appeal 'almost exactly met the bills' for the architect's plans and preliminary work. At the launch party, Colum spoke of how, clearing up in the Lodge the night before, he had found a pound on the floor. 'That is a very important pound', he said: 'because it's a prototype! It is a very special pound to set your imagination racing. It's a start to the really big appeal: from today, we're in business with our team of architects and surveyors.'

The mountain was now fully in view, summit and all … but with one awful long way still to climb.

At New Lands, group leaders from the Americas, Australia, Africa and Europe gathered for a conference to meditate, share experiences and learn together. In London, however, there were rather different scenes, as a giant storm broke over the leaky roof, and a deluge came soaking into the chapels and gallery, ruining carpets and bringing down part of the ceiling. Two inches of water covered the floor of the main chapel. The London brothers knew that the hard work was only just beginning, as they stood 'very wet and in various stages of undress, to send out the light at 6 pm!' However the flood provided renewed inspiration. Colum wrote 'whatever the causes of the flood, we took it to be as clear a symbol as could be that those above wanted us to press ahead with getting a building that would withstand the onslaught of the elements!' The urgency of the appeal now led to the launch of the 'Bricks of Light' scheme as friends and Brothers were urged to purchase their own symbolic brick to help to build the new London Lodge.

Heart of England sponsored walk, 1994

Of course, our British centres were not alone in their hard work, and the London Lodge plans were not Minesta's only hundredth birthday present. 'Gifts' were offered from across the world. The new Australian retreat centre was scheduled to open its doors at almost exactly the time of Minesta's birthday and was truly a magnificent tribute. More and more it had become needed, to accommodate the demand for places on retreats. Then in early 1992 Joan Rasmussen, a brother who previously had opened her home to accommodate retreat participants, fell ill. This was the final impetus to go ahead with the plans and construction. After the builders finished, a wonderful team of volunteers cleaned and prepared the centre ready to welcome its first occupants. Their work was completed just the week before the Retreats were scheduled to commence.

Outside the Retreat Centre bedrooms is a fragrant flowerbed allowing the gentle breezes to carry the perfume of roses, violets and alyssum into the rooms. Lush, sub-tropical gardens surround the whole complex, lovingly tended by a very caring group of dedicated gardeners. Jenny, visiting the following year, reported back that 'words cannot do justice to it. It makes full use of the large spectacular site with large picture windows looking down the valley, and beautiful furnishings. Each bedroom has its own name and colour scheme'. The retreat centre at Maleny remains a most lovely place to stay and is a real monument to the dedication of the workers who truly created it out of spirit vision, whether by hard work (there was lots of that!) or by financial sacrifice.

Nearing completion: the Retreat Centre at Maleny

*

The final and most spectacular gift was yet to come, but it was not achieved without sorrow and difficulty. Our earlier report (pp. 115–6) spoke of the plan to build, on what had always been known as the

One of the more recent trailers on the Texas land

Retreat Center Land in Texas, a new building to house participants in retreats and host speaker meetings, and then a temple for worship. It may here be added that up to this point, any overnight visitor simply had a bedroom in a 'trailer' – what in Britain we would think of as something between a large caravan and a mobile home. Given the climate and wood-eating pests in Texas, these trailers do not last for very long, and although mention of them stirs remarkably happy memories, they were not (can we say it without offending anyone?) of five-star standard! At the same time they added wonderfully to the sense of pioneering that was such a feature of the work in the Americas at the time.

There was always a plan to build a temple there eventually – the map of the land itself gave a proposed site for that, well set back into the grounds – but for the moment it seemed as though the retreat accommodation was more urgent, and that the extra accommodation would itself help to raise funds for a later temple. From an earthly point of view this seemed sensible, and initially from a 'guidance' point of view as well. The project was exciting, too: an early design featured a pyramid construction and a great deal of imaginative investment was tied up in the plan. Progressively, though, it felt to be the wrong way round: that investing in accommodation which would permit talks and study as well as retreat, before the place of worship was to put the mind and maybe the purse before the heart and the spirit. There was deep discussion of this throughout the summer of 1991, involving both the Mother Lodge in England and the local brothers and leaders, and culminating in a visit by Geoffrey Dent to Texas in October 1991. Right to the final moment there was confusion, uncertainty, debate.

It was actually a vision received from Michael Collishaw in England, a UK Trustee of the work but a member of the US Board as well, which at last brought illumination and release from a somewhat agonising period. Michael's vision of the Temple, with the Retreat Center programmed to follow very shortly after, seemed to carry such wisdom that it carried everyone with it. Like Radiance before him, Michael had had a distinguished career in the Civil Service. One might think that this gave their wisdom a worldly connotation, yet it is probably truer to say that the very best training in the world brings not a narrowness of mind but such a breadth as to give room for the immenseness of inspiration that a work such as White Eagle's sometimes needs.

Once the right plan was on the table, things moved fast, and so it was that at the time of Minesta's centenary the Temple of the Golden Rose in America was already nearing completion. It would become the third White Eagle Temple worldwide and, as STELLA POLARIS pointed out, 'a point of power on a great triangle of light'. Jean LeFevre said during the construction process: 'we are doing it

Michael Collishaw

together: the Temple is really here, and you have made this miracle happen. It is built through faith and the power of love. We believe the Temple of the Golden Rose will be exquisite. White Eagle so often speaks of the fragrance of the rose: may this truly be a Temple through which the light of Christ may manifest to the earth – bringing peace and healing to all life.'

The opening of the Temple was scheduled to be carried out on 25 October 1992 – just a year after the final decision to build it had been taken – and was to be jointly performed by Jean LeFevre, Mother of the American White Eagle work, and Joan Hodgson, overall Lodge Mother, who at the age of 79 was to make a special trip from England, supported by members of her family. Joan and Jean would address a congregation swollen by brothers from Australia, South Africa, West Africa, England and Japan, as well as those from at least fifteen American States. It was the most international gathering that had ever been seen in the White Eagle work.

The fight to complete on time!

But the chosen date was, let us say, courageous. An ever-increasing team of builders and volunteer helpers worked with Jean and her husband, John, determined to complete their mammoth task in time for the opening ceremony. STELLA POLARIS reported that: 'As the days pass, the Temple grows. The exterior lining of the dome disappears under its finishing sheets of copper. The wooden frame is covered with insulation. What looked like useful loft space disappears as miles of air conditioning tubes are squeezed into it. Will it be ready for October?... it will be a close-run thing.'

Close ... and yet, miraculously, they managed it. The entire site was landscaped 'in a matter of a few days' by a party of volunteers. Another party scrubbed the chairs. In the weeks previously, twenty choir robes were made by one volunteer, and the choir itself was described as seeming 'to come forth from nothing, like a shoot from a dry bulb'. At last, the magical readiness was achieved, and the Temple was ready, an example of faith and the effort of moving many mountains. From STELLA POLARIS: 'The temple is a soft yellow within. The carpet is gentle amethyst. The chairs are white ... we seated 75 in one great circle. The altar is simple, white, and on it stands a Celtic cross from Iona... Behind are five stained glass windows, made by a local friend. One features the Lodge symbol while the others represent the four elements in beautiful colours.'

Ready for inspection...

Joan and Jean walked into the new Temple at 3 pm on 25 October, to dedicate the Temple to God and the Universal Brotherhood of life. Colum wrote at the time that 'the sense of the other world was almost palpable.' In retrospect now, he adds this comment. 'I went out to Texas early, and have particularly strong memories of the landscaping work beforehand ... particularly of the struggles of lifting clods of earth thick with the most painfully-biting ants. There was a wonderful spirit among the volunteers, though. Perhaps indicative of the

THE STORY OF THE WHITE EAGLE LODGE

…and open!

fight we had to get everything done (and a reminder of all the difficulties earlier), the planet Mars, with its rosy tint, seemed to stand guard over us. I remember the absolute magic, though, of looking up into a liquid blue sky as night replaced twilight, and the huge visiting party, after the opening was performed, sat down to supper. There, feeling as though it had actually replaced Mars, was shining down upon us the clear still influence of Venus, planet of harmony.'

A great deal of travelling for Grace Cooke's family also occurred in her centenary year; in July, Jeremy Hayward and his new wife, Anna, travelled to Germany for the opening of the White Eagle centre in Munich. Annemarie Libera, the warm and inspirational leader of the White Eagle work in Germany, had taken over from Jana Faust, the original leader, and she welcomed them to the opening ceremony, which was also attended by fifty others. Anna wrote that 'the beautiful small chapel was filled and overflowing with people and with love…. The house is on a hill and looks out across village rooftops to a beautiful valley, and so across woods and fields to the mountains. On the final evening the Bavarian Alps were for the first time standing out in a beautiful clear light, and it seems like a blessing to us all on our way home. As the last person left, the house returned to stillness and the angels seemed to fold their wings around it; and among the flowers, there in the gloaming, were the bright, brief dances of the fireflies. So even in the darkness the light shines – and each one of our friends in Germany and indeed all over the world is like an eternal firefly, and each centre for the work is like a home for all our individual lights, where we can blend and grow together and serve as one.'

Special moment: at the Stockport group leaders Eric and Shirley Warrington celebrate twenty years of leadership,, 1975–1995

CHAPTER VII
A Worldwide Work of Healing

IN THE YEARS following Minesta's centenary, the worldwide growth of the work that she had begun continued to accelerate. The 1990s were rich years! In 1993, Jenny and Geoffrey visited Switzerland and stayed with Carol Sommer, the new leader of the work there, for the opening of the new centre. Jenny conducted the dedication service (which was attended by ninety people) and described the day.

'Our White Eagle centre is in Burgdorf, a small country town surrounded by soft green hills with a distant view of the Alps, and it is furnished in white and soft pink, with large windows which open onto the 'heavenly' garden, complete with lotus pond, fountain, rose bower and white seat. The chapel itself has such a lovely atmosphere already that on entering one feels as though one is walking into a rose sanctuary in the world of light. On the white altar there are just flowers and the simple grail cup, as in the New Lands Temple. For the Dedication Day we were blessed by warm, unbroken sunshine, so everyone could enjoy the earthly garden as well as the heavenly one.'

Opening of the new Swiss centre at Burgdorf

Jenny and Geoffrey were particularly pleased to be joined in Burgdorf by Walter and Edith Ohr and Trudi Keller, tireless workers for the light in Switzerland for so many years, and group leaders since the 1950s. They had handed their work over to Carol to continue it. Walter was blind for much of his life, and his wife Edith his full-time carer, so their achievement was an example to all of us. Trudi, his sister, spent many years in the London Lodge in the 1960s and 1970s, while Walter and Edith were familiar visitors on New Lands retreats. Their work with translating the teaching is described elsewhere. Another Swiss pioneer and translator, but in the French-speaking part (she ran a small White Eagle group in Lausanne) was Odette Sotoudeh. All of those named except Carol today continue their service from the world of light, helping and guiding Carol and her faithful brothers and supporters.

The years following the opening at Burgdorf have emphasised the dedication of our family in Switzerland, as they have demonstrated their ability to 'keep on keeping on' in the face of various challenges, including having to change their home several times

Michael Collishaw conducts a meeting in the Netherlands with Marga van Velsen

Preparing the ground: Patricia Fletcher with the first leaders of the work in South Africa, David and Betty Smith; and at Table Mountain, which in 1994 so impressed Jenny

(they are presently in Emmental). Undeterred, their faith shines strong. In Jenny's words, 'Wherever they are, a beautiful spiritual centre and warm, loving, physical space is created for White Eagle's family in Switzerland'.

The White Eagle work has flourished in many areas of Europe in recent times, and in the Netherlands a particularly dedicated group of brothers have been meeting for many years. In 1994 a happy and successful retreat day was held in Breda, a beautiful city in Brabant province. The peace and stillness during the retreat was seen as a 'living symbol of the presence of the unseen brethren' while those on the earth plane were also numerous. 150 attended, testimony to the importance of the White Eagle work in the Netherlands, where twenty different groups in all parts of the country were continuing to work for the light. The Breda retreat was one in a series of retreats in which our brothers in the Netherlands continued their White Eagle work, often aided by Michael Collishaw, who was deeply committed to his work in the Netherlands with our Dutch brethren and who also led retreats for more than fifty in Belgium.

This expansion in the Netherlands was highlighted in 1995 when Jeremy and Anna Hayward visited to run a retreat and contact healing course near Amsterdam. Jeremy and Anna joined the leaders of the work in Holland (Britta Hudig, assisted by Diny Hartman and Marga Van Velsen) to enjoy a 'very beautiful family atmosphere, with opportunities for support of each other, sharing and much fun.... Jeremy and Anna took home with them, as a gift, a long string of bulbs which will grace the gardens at New Lands, providing yet another earthly link for our sense of being one united family worldwide, as well as in spirit'.

Noteworthy development was not confined to Europe, however. A Daughter Lodge and Centre for Canada opened in Toronto, led by Pat Harrison and with Jean LeFevre and Colum Hayward present.

Jenny visited South Africa in 1994, carrying out retreats in Cape Town and Durban. Staying with South African brothers Evelyn Van Vloten and Maybelle van Warmelo, and meeting over seventy friends at various events including a 'magical time of meditation on Table Mountain', Jenny was greatly struck by the importance of the growing work in Africa – she felt a 'light-power' in the very earth itself which is bringing an increasing awareness of brotherly love to the whole of Africa'. The vision had particular significance for Jenny, who vowed to continue her personal involvement with spreading the light throughout Africa.

The relevance of Jenny's vision for the whole of Africa became increasingly clear as the work in West Africa also expanded rapidly, with many different groups flourishing in the face of extremely difficult conditions and despite the financial and cultural issues faced by West African members. We spoke of some of the early pioneers;

another was Regina Olajolo, who had offered herself for training in the London Lodge earlier. Further east, one of the most pioneering of the group leaders there, Paul Njotu, from Cameroon, wrote in 1994 about the 'wonderful celebration and feast that was held for the second anniversary of the Cameroon group'. Paul gave a talk which appeared in the newspapers and was read over the local and national news, raising the profile of the White Eagle work in West Africa in a wonderful way and assuring his country that 'our work is to engulf the African continent in peace, through healing prayer and love in action'. An inspiring testament.

Inner Peaceville: early Lagos White Eagle Centre

*

The Golden Mountain Appeal caught the worldwide community's imagination and parts were played by members the world over. Small deeds and larger ones gathered together to achieve miracles is the story of how White Eagle members managed to raise funds for the new London Lodge. In a kaleidoscope of colourful and lively ways, our friends and brothers raised a great amount of money. It would not be possible to list the effort of every individual worker for the light – we would need an entire additional volume for that! – but here are a selected few…

Individuals made sterling efforts: Christa Forbes, a redoubtable fundraiser at New Lands, made enough recycled greetings cards to raise the almost unbelievable sum of £3,000 by 1995. Letchworth member Jeanette White raised over £100 with a parachute jump. Jenny Dent swam 5000 metres in a sponsored swim, while in Sydney, Australia, Lyndy Abraham held a piano recital for the appeal. In the London Lodge itself, a 'hugely enjoyable' Promises Auction, followed by a cookery demonstration by Rose Elliot, raised £1,900. Peter Greenhill made a memorable auctioneer.

Scenes from 'Cinderella'

Most ambitious, a witty take on 'Cinderella' was performed later in the year, and brought together a wonderful array of talent, including a lively contribution from the younger members of the London Lodge, under the direction of Sandra Coates. Professional training paid off in the leading roles: singer Catherine Fenton as Cinderella and dance critic Giannandrea Poesio as Prince Charming. It was probably the most ambitious piece of theatre ever performed in the London Lodge, despite a noble pedigree which includes Brother Faithful's memorable masque, 'Our Brother the Sun' years before (actually in 1943), and the regular Christmas entertainments of Edna Taylor and the Eaglets in the 1960s and 1970s (over which those who remember them still chuckle from time to time!).

As if that level of ambition wasn't enough, perhaps the most courageous event of all came with the opening of an exhibition of over fifty artists' work, entitled 'An Open Window' (1994). We had long noticed how many artists we had in the Lodge, some of them not

Art Exhibition, London 1994

We made the top!

without reputation in the world. Their generosity in giving pictures or in taking only a small percentage, was more unexpected. Jennie Harding, who had also managed the Promises Auction, took the weight of organising it, and the exhibition filled the Main Chapel and the Gallery upstairs for two weeks, while services continued in the Brotherhood Chapel. Jeremy wrote that 'many of the pictures began to speak to us as we lived with them: to speak of some richness and beauty found in the human heart by the artist out of their life's experience … the energy in the chapel felt to me a most warm and uplifted one'. It was a particularly appropriate fundraising event when we remember the London Lodge's previous life as an artist's studio!

Out and about across Britain (literally), eleven walkers took part in a three-day climb across the peaks of the Lake District and raised over £4,000 in just one of the many fundraising sponsored walks that took place over the whole country (our Yorkshire brethren were particularly supportive). Concerts and slide shows and talks were held. And at the New Lands Summer Festival, an enormous Grand Draw was held, with prizes including a week in Paris, and it raised £4,300 for the appeal.

THE STORY OF THE WHITE EAGLE LODGE   123

'The fundraising for the London Lodge was the most "fun" of all our appeals, I think (Colum writes today) but it was also the most exhausting. Not only in human terms. The upheaval mentioned, around the art exhibition, was a case in point. Actually to rebuild the London Lodge was a vast, vast, project. Maybe it was too ambitious; I don't know. We felt that the inspiration was genuine, but a huge task was set them, and the London Lodge brothers began to tire. We were still a long, long way from completion of fundraising: when would construction start? Had we set for ourselves a trap out of which there was no way except to wait, and wait, in faith?

Eileen Walters, ideal receptionist

'It was a moment when the London brothers themselves came to the fore, and said to us, enough is enough. They understood that the exhaustion that all felt was too great a price to pay for the new building. Although the decision was ultimately one for the Lodge Mother and the Trustees, the voice of the Brotherhood was impossible to ignore. For the best spiritual reasons, it had to be followed. I can't say that it was the easiest moment of my life. I had taken up the torch from Joan in leading the appeal, and it should have felt like crushing defeat. Actually, I don't think it was, or even that it truly felt so at the time. Although we lost our vision of a landmark building, the sense that the Brotherhood themselves had come together, taken a decision at great cost to themselves, and then presented it to their leaders, actually felt like a gift, and deep down inside I do not think that the wrong course is ever taken (though I review this position every time the roof leaks, still!). At the time, I wrote the following in STELLA POLARIS, this time meaning the spiritual Brotherhood rather than the earthly one:

"We must always have a vision…. The Brotherhood help us to have our vision, and yet if it is not meant to be, we know that there is something better, more appropriate, waiting for us. We have to flow with the will of God, and trust in the Divine Plan, whilst doing our best to follow our inner guidance.'

Brotherhood altar in the old Lodge

And so, with a lessened ideal – a very substantial refurbishment of the existing building – the summit of that London's Golden Mountain was reached at last. New plans were drawn up with Building Surveyors that were exciting in themselves. Elements, such as the semi-circular alcove protecting the altar in the main chapel, took their cue from the abandoned design. STELLA POLARIS reported that 'We hope and believe that the final scheme … will still beautifully meet our needs, and we know that, when a decision is issued from an apparently human source, in reality it is the brothers in spirit urging us on, either to rethink that aspect or subtly to change it in a way we had not envisaged.' In the summer of 1995 work at last began (although the fundraising, even for refurbishment, was set to continue until 1997) and the London Lodge was closed for six months for renovation.

Last service before the refurbishment; the fireplace discovered behind the altar; chapel created in the home of Anne and Monique during the closure

The time of rebuilding was one of mixed emotions – a mixture of excitement as the plans, so long dreamed of, began to be put in place combined with sadness at seeing the London Lodge closed and stripped down to 'a shell' by mid-September. In STELLA POLARIS we noted how with 'the sound of drilling, the sound of radios, there is a busy-ness of a different sort than we are used to. New partitions arise, unfamiliar. With outward eyes, there is little to remind you of 'our Lodge'. Here is Colum again: 'I have never been so aware as in its "absence" of how the London Lodge is not the building. I know now that its "presence" is all the more real in this transition than ever it was.' Staff and volunteers worked hard during the closure, surrounded by dust and hard hats, trying to make sure that the new building would fulfil the dreams of so many.

It must have been a bit like after the bombing, when services continued in Edinburgh, for the spirit of the London Lodge continued to exist, and faithful brothers, particularly Monique Regester and Anne Cornock-Taylor (Sister White Rose and Sister Diana) held meetings in their own homes. Coach trips were organised to carry Londoners to major services at New Lands. Hopes were that the new Lodge would be open by Christmas – STELLA POLARIS asked for donations for the Christmas Fair to be handed in as usual, but to New Lands – but, as so often in the world of building works, these hopes proved unrealisable. 'We are all a little sad to miss the Christmas activities', Colum wrote 'but the building work has, in the end, taken us to a higher standard of refurbishment than we could have thought possible, and if the cost is in the extra time, it will have been worth it.'

The London Lodge finally reopened on Sunday, 21 January 1996. It had been 'an epic job' getting everything ready, but the results were well worth it. When they saw the reopened Lodge visitors were stunned by its beauty, particularly the redesigned main chapel with its altar surmounted by an arching canopy. Colum wrote 'The altar in the main chapel seemed to symbolise wings of light reaching out to enfold everyone present, and yet, at the same time, creating a sense of depth into which each one was drawn, closer and closer, to the spiritual life'. The main chapel was illuminated by arched windows looking down from an elegantly enlarged gallery above, leading to a breathtakingly silent, domed Brotherhood chapel. The library was also particularly striking, combining modern freshness with a classical, traditional elegance. Nigel Millross, who had given a large number of inspirational ideas, had insisted we move the huge wooden fire surround up from the old main chapel to the library, to make it feel pleasantly domestic. It worked. All these delights were ready to be inspected at the time of the Lodge's Diamond Jubilee with a two-day celebration incorporating a glorious concert, and at a grand open day in May that was attended by 120 people.

Tribute is due to Chryssa Porter, and to her husband, David, a leading Quantity Surveyor, for their work and sacrifice at the time of the refurbishment. The later creation of a new office in the London Lodge (1998–9) was project-managed very efficiently by Nigel Millross, who had shown such originality in the refurbishment. In the refurbished Lodge, a new team took over. Eileen Walters (pictured on p. 124), who had greeted an incredible number of people as they came into the Lodge gave way to dear new helpers such as the efficient Pearl Satchell (now Rauberts) and the always-humorous Gefry Horrabbin. The London Lodge is much indebted to all such, for the quality of work and atmosphere in what was quite a 'golden age' in its history.

Recreated!

*

Pearl and Gefry

Our beloved Lodge Mother, Joan Hodgson, was diagnosed with a form of leukaemia in 1994. With this news, she began a genuinely inspirational journey. Doctors had thought that Joan's leukaemia would take her from her physical body in a matter of weeks, but she remained in her physical body for a further eighteen months, an extraordinary testament to the power of spiritual healing. They were wonderful months, too, allowing Joan's family to come to terms with her illness and to deepen the heart-to-heart contact that has continued since she passed. As she had done since the days of Burstow Manor, she set a lasting example for us all. Joan faced the reality of her own death with acceptance and dignity, nurtured by the deep connection she felt with the world of spirit, which deepened as the months passed. At peace with her life and her work, she was filled with joy to be rejoining her beloved husband, John, five years after his sudden passing to the world of light.

Joan continued to work as Lodge Mother, jointly with Ylana, in the months after her diagnosis, despite her illness. Jeremy, part of whose work lay with recordings, once described the tape of the talk and meditation that she gave at the Group Leaders' Conference in the summer of 1994. 'This was shortly after the leukaemia had been diagnosed and her physical body was quite weak. However, of all the recordings to which I listened, from services and talks over the years, this is the one which actually feels to me to have most lightness of heart, the deepest inner feeling of trust in life and death. This lightness of feeling as she approached her transition is to me another precious gift, which I hope will be a touchstone of wisdom for many of us in future years.'

Joan with Eunice, Sister Love

Margot Kemhadjian

Joan's nurse throughout all the final months was Eunice Watson, to whom an enormous debt of gratitude is owed her for her cheerfulness, patience and practicality. This also feels an appropriate place to record a tribute to Margot Kemhadjian, who gave Joan so much care and companionship after John's passing. One of the few who at the end of the twentieth century could still just remember Pembroke Hall, Margot also gave sterling service in countless ways in New Lands offices, after her retirement from UNICEF in Paris.

The time of Joan's passing was a particularly special one as, with her wide and extended family at her bedside, she talked of her final wishes. Joan's family were all-important to her. She had been so happy to be able to attend the wedding of her granddaughter, Sara, to Joseph Cody in July 1995 – one of her last outings – and, some weeks later, looking out of her bedroom window at the glorious roses that had been her husband John's pride and joy, she spoke to Joe and asked him to build her a garden.

'Circles of pink and white roses … a garden of meditation and communion.' Joan gave specific instructions, and Joe, a Royal Horticultural Society-trained garderner and landscaper – who had already created the wildflower meadows that added such beauty to Temple Hill – began to draw up plans for the Garden of Communion, an enclosed garden opening out of the Temple on the side of

the hill, a place to remember the gifts Joan gave to us all.

Joan dedicated her life totally to White Eagle's work except for a spell in youth spent teaching, and with that gift she gave her great intelligence, wisdom, and spiritual power. An extraordinary healer, she was also the kindest and most caring of people, with warmth that flooded through her like sunshine to all who came to her for help. After Joan's passing, letters flooded in from people who had been touched by her love and care over her many years of service. Lyn Commins, now Edwards, wrote from Australia: 'What I will always remember is the absolute beauty of her presence. She was so kind, so gentle and yet so simple and humble.… That was the feeling, the presence that was with her all the time: that of this wonderful, wise, old soul'.

Nancie Patterson, co-leader of the Ontario Daughter Lodge in

Joan's other focus in the work was on the teaching of children. HULLO SUN, *published in 1972, remains in print*

Canada, wrote: 'The last time I saw Joan was at the dedication of the Temple in Texas. Unfortunately, I was taken ill, and she brought me a chair, sat me in it, and stayed talking quietly to me until I recovered. In the midst of her public life she still had time to stop and look after the fallen sparrow. Her life was given to the work of expressing the beauty and eternal truths which White Eagle sent to us all.'

A Danish brother wrote: 'We feel joy because we know that Joan is happy now with her John, and as White Eagle says, 'all is good'…. When I think of her, I have the most wonderful picture in my heart of Joan and John walking hand in hand, laughing and smiling in the sunlight. And I know this is the way it is.'

The feelings of all were summed up by these words in STELLA POLARIS: 'Thank you Joan, for your love for us all. For the wisdom you have embodied for us all by how you lived your life, with all its human experience. Thank you for showing us how to walk forward into the light with a heart full of equanimity.'

The Council of the White Eagle School of Astrology meets with Jenny around the round table in the Brotherhood Library

One of Joan's many gifts to the White Eagle work was the School of Astrology, which was constituted under her leadership in 1976, although her first astrological book, WISDOM IN THE STARS, had been published as early as 1943, and she had offered White Eagle astrology courses long before 1976. From her personal study as an astrologer, almost entirely self-taught but much influenced by Alan Leo (she worked with Margaret Hone also), Joan built up the School, which was taken over and ably led by Simon Bentley after her passing. In the years after Joan's passing we feel sure she has watched with pride and pleasure the progress of the study that she began. The School gained official recognition and acclaim from

IN WEST AFRICA

Hamida (front left) and Frederick (back, second from left) Bote-Kwame have through a series of visits from London successfully co-ordinated the White Eagle work in West Africa. In the picture above John Okonkwo, whose links with the Lodge go back nearly forty years, stands at the back on the left. Below left, the central figure in traditional dress is Professor Jones Babalola who has had links almost as long; while the newly-initiated Brother bottom right is Prosper Agbenkey. For a full key, see p. 160.

THE STORY OF THE WHITE EAGLE LODGE

Adding some colour! Fred and Hamida were married in the London Lodge. On the right is Brown Songhonron, one of the present Mother Lodge Trustees

Britta Hudig

astrological experts, having been officially recognised by the new Advisory panel on Astrological Education. The number of students has grown steadily year by year, and the school's popularity around the world continues to increase, becoming truly international, with Simon now regularly leading astrological retreats and lectures in America and Australia.

Meanwhile, Jenny's vision of the development of the work in Africa was given special confirmation in 1999 when Hamida Bote-Kwame and her husband Frederick, both stalwart members of the London Lodge, visited the network of groups in West Africa. Fred was born in Ghana and Hamida in Nigeria, and so had a unique ability to bridge communities and continents. The local West African members had been an inspiration to all for many years: unable to buy books because of lack of access to English money, suffering from many local difficulties, they had nevertheless striven and worked faithfully for the light, often in very difficult conditions and circumstances and with little contact with each other.

It was with an aim to help to establish a greater local contact that Hamida and Fred wrote that their 'mission was to take encouragement to and to network the groups in West Africa'. Travelling first to Ghana, they found 'a dedicated and buoyant group who meet thrice weekly for discussions of the teachings and for service'; run by Evelyn Addy, and her father, Robert, a follower of the teaching since the 1960s. They also visited several groups in Nigeria, where they travelled with the leader of the work in the region, Maxwell Mbene. Hamida wrote that 'the period was truly as test of faith for us, for our visits were mostly unexpected, there was no means of phone communication, letters were not received before our arrival and the roads were treacherous in some cases. Nevertheless, all the groups leaders, unknown to each other, recounted miraculous experience of how they had been kept at home on the days of our visits.... Throughout the visits we were greatly humbled by the dedication of the different members, despite the austerity of their economic conditions ... a bright light in the heart of their continent'.

The White Eagle work was continuing to expand in the Netherlands, and Britta Hudig described how 'people from the Netherlands, Germany and Belgium come together, bringing a true feeling of how boundaries fall away, and how true brotherhood will be in the New Age' The workers in the Netherlands met at 'a small convent in Tiltenburg' but, as Britta wrote, 'meanwhile, we are saving for our new centre, which we do not have, and we are learning to use our thought-power to create this centre together; not just a physical centre, but one of true brotherhood and of harmony in our hearts'.

This beautiful process of visualisation and work towards harmony linked with happy news from Denmark, where years of the same sort of visualisation and prayer had culminated in the opening of a long-awaited new centre there. Grethe Fremming, Rolf Haus-bol and Kirsten Thomsen began their work in Denmark in 1981 and had envisaged their own centre for years when all of a sudden, in Grethe's words, 'the centre … found us! It is situated in the most soft green nature, surrounded by preserved areas, down to the sea'. The building, an old farmhouse, is set in miles of gentle, hilly green countryside outside Copenhagen and was named the Polaris Centre, after guidance from White Eagle led them to a passage in the book PLANETARY HARMONIES. One notable feature of the Polaris Centre is a stone monolith on the land, bearing a cross within the circle design.

The first five-day retreat was held in Denmark in 1989 (top). The lower picture shows another retreat, held in Copenhagen in 1992

In June 1999 Jenny travelled to Denmark to carry out the official opening of the new centre, writing that there was 'a feeling of light all the way on the drive to the Polaris Centre, and I was thrilled with everything I saw. Because as yet there is only a relatively small sanctuary, Grethe had arranged for a blue and white marquee to be erected and transformed into our Temple for the weekend. It was truly a miracle in miniature, complete with a main altar with a grail cup and flowers at either side, just like our Temple here at New Lands. The only drawback of this beautiful Temple of Light was that when it rained – and it did from time to time! – the sound of the rain was quite loud; it truly felt as if we were in an open-air temple at times. The angels of the elements were very close, and I was reminded of their blessing at the time of the Temple opening service in June 1974. Over a hundred people attended the dedication service, on Saturday afternoon, 5 June, and we completed with a "party" and the giving and unwrapping of gifts for the Centre from many well-wishers, including friends from other European countries'.

This joy of visualising and creating something lovely in itself was echoed in October, 1997 when the new Daughter Lodge in Germany was dedicated (it had moved from its first home, mentioned on p. 119). The centre, at beautiful Lake Wessling, came about, once again, as a result of many years of tireless work by Annemarie Libera and her fellow brothers. The dedication service, led by Jeremy and Anna Hayward, was described as a time of 'celebration, reaffirmation and healing,' with a 'strong and powerful feeling of brotherhood' and was attended by more than fifty people. Once again, it was heartwarming to see brothers present from elsewhere in Europe.

Annemarie and Johannes

The work of the centre continued to expand over the years that followed, continuing to develop and unfold in many beautiful ways. The hard work of Annemarie and her talented husband, Johannes, has enabled great progress in Germany, including official recognition and tax-free status being provided by the German authorities, and the establishment of a publishing company, 'Stella Polaris Verlag', to print German translations of the White Eagle books and the magazine STELLA POLARIS, with the profits benefiting Lodge funds.

International leaders' gathering at the New Lands Temple in the early 1990s. Diny Hartman, mentioned in the text here, is the central figure in the front row

Opening of the new Star Centre at Limburg in the South Netherlands by Jenny, May 2005

Expansion in other areas of Europe was also dramatic. In a beautiful confirmation of faith, just two years after Britta Hudig wrote that the brothers in the Netherlands were using their power of thought to create their centre, the White Eagle Centre in Den Haag opened its doors. Britta retired as leader of the work in the Netherlands in 1999, after many years of wonderful service, and her successor Diny Hartman led the work in the Netherlands from the centre in Den Haag, where she lived. Diny wrote that it was 'touching to see fifty-seven people all together as one warm family, the youngest only two months old and the eldest over eighty-three years! The Den Haag group has been inspired and guided to this home … and so many of the groups members helped, somehow or other, to make a vision come true. We are so grateful to everyone for all those gifts of love. Apart from the chapel (created by joining two rooms together, so that it can seat sixty) the centre contains a kitchen and an office and, last but not least, a lovely terrace. On that terrace we've met four new friends – a seagull, a pigeon, and two jackdaws. Jonathan, the gull, is in the habit of knocking on the kitchen window to draw our attention, thus inviting us to offer him his daily bread.… Except for a coat of paint, we've settled into our new centre. As from now all activities of the Hague group will be held here and by way of service we hope to turn our centre every more into one from which the light will radiate throughout the world.'

Developing this theme when dedicating the centre in 2000, Jenny likened the plan for the worldwide White Eagle work to a golden tapestry of light, its beauty gradually revealed as many brothers and sisters weave their threads. Jenny also paid tribute to the service done by Britta and Diny over the years in developing the work in the Netherlands. This work in the Netherlands was to strengthen even further in subsequent years, with the dedication of a second centre, a Daughter Lodge for the South, on 8 May 2005. This was to be ably led by Marga van Velsen, who had looked after the work there for many years, and who took over as leader for the country as a whole when Diny retired in 2003, so that the dedication that day was also a rededication for the Star Centre for the Netherlands.

*

This wonderful expansion and development of new centres was not confined to Europe, however. In 1999 Jenny went again to Australia, this time to dedicate the new Sydney Daughter Lodge. On this occasion, the Lodge was based not in a physical 'centre' but in the beautiful home of a sister, Phyllis Geissler. Jenny emphasised its spiritual strength in a clear message she received from spirit: 'a Daughter Lodge is not actually a physical building, but rather, a strong, clear light which is nurtured by all, its brothers, healers and members, a grail cup of light on the inner planes'. It was a particularly significant moment for the Australian Lodge, as the work had been begun very early on by a dedicated lone worker, Winifred Browne, but the first group had been in Sydney, meeting from 1961. The work had been 'nurtured' over the years by many faithful workers for the light in and around Sydney before Queensland took over as the main centre. It was a notable achievement to be able to make a new dedication in the city, thus recognising it as one of the original centres for the light.

Jenny of course visited the Temple at Maleny too, where she paid tribute to the hard work of Doris and Alf Commins' daughters, Gay and Lyn, who have continued to lead the work in Australia, supported still, as we write in 2008, by the motherly guidance of Doris. Alf passed into the world of light in 1997 after many years of service. A simple farmer at heart, Alf had brought wisdom and much human 'backbone' in every sense of the word. There is a further photograph of him on p. 96. Lyn married Steve Edwards in 1994, and Steve has since become one of the stalwart workers at the Temple, devoting his many talents to supporting Lyn and her family, and creating what Jenny described as 'a quartet of wonderful workers who have guided the work not only of the Temple, but of all of Australasia'. Typically, when they read proofs of this book, Gay and Lyn wanted to make absolutely sure that any praise was extended out to include every hardworking participant in the work there. They are, we have found on visiting, a remarkable team at all levels.

The Commins family. Alf is in the front, alongside Doris and with Gay on his other side. Lyn and Steve stand behind

While on the subject of teamwork, another not very public development is worth mentioning, although the pioneering work for this was done in the Americas. It was felt from spirit that the work would be well served by instituting there a Council of Brothers, consultative rather than executive, who would review policies, suggest initiatives and stand as a spiritual reference lest at any stage the work needed better landmarks. Membership would be rotating, giving as many brothers as possible the opportunity to serve. So successful has this Council been in the Americas (sometimes brimming with ideas and talent!) that the experiment has been copied in the UK and in Australasia. The latter is the most recently formed – in May 2007 only – but as Lyn and Gay told us while commenting on 'the team', those Council members, even in twelve months, 'have come up with very productive ideas'.

In the Americas, there was pleasing growth and development in the work in 1999. A new Daughter Lodge in Vancouver, British Columbia, was dedicated in the autumn (fall!) – by Colum Hayward (scarcely out of plaster from a serious mountaineering accident), Pat Harrison (Canada White Eagle leader) and Jean LeFevre. It represented the culmination of untiring work by a team of White

Canada: opening of the Surrey, BC, Daughter Lodge. Colum, Pat Harrison, Jane Sorbi, Jean LeFevvre, Ann Force, Clive Steyning

Eagle workers led by Anne Force and was to meet in a former Spiritualist Church.

At Montgomery, Texas, there was also a major development that year: the time had come to get on with building the Retreat Home. Jenny visited the Temple of the Golden Rose in March and was struck by the beauty of the surroundings: 'the Texan countryside and roadside is bright with glorious wildflowers – bluebonnets, Indian paintbrushes, blue-eyed grass, blue vetch and many varieties of golden daisies which open wide in the midday sun.… I enjoyed some lovely walks, listening to the song of many birds'. Nature is certainly an important part of the Texan centre. Jean LeFevre described the vision for the centre as being a sanctuary 'not only for wildlife, but a sanctuary from all the pressures of the outer world, for human beings too. On a retreat there is time to walk the land and enjoy the beauty round you, or simply to sit. There are places of stillness where benches invite you to rest and read a White Eagle meditation from a star-shaped board. One of the special pleasures is to enjoy the magnificent sunset, when the sun glistens on the golden bronze doors of the Temple.'

The vision for the work in the Americas had been a brave one; as Jean said: 'In 1982, we had less than one hundred supporters and no financial resources. Acquiring the acres of land, building the Temple of the Golden Rose, and now building the Retreat Home, have all been acts of faith'. They were acts, however, that proved well justified. As 1999 continued, the building of the Retreat Center building commenced, with a blessing when the first land was dug, on 18 July.

Yet while they emphasised growth in North America, the last years of the Millennium truly emphasised the great cycle of life, birth and death for Grace Cooke's family. Jenny and Geoffrey Dent's marriage had ended, yet they remained the closest of friends and their family stayed almost as closely united as before, setting a genuine example of how unconditional love can transcend and outlast life's difficulties. In 1998, renewed happiness was brought to Geoffrey's family life when he married Melanie Bassett, who, living in Bath, had been for many years a brother of the Lodge. The beautiful service in the Temple introduced her to a new life at New Lands, bringing many gifts of warmth, love and talents with her. Further family celebration occurred the next year as Michael Dent returned from voluntary work overseas just in time to greet his new niece, Daisy Grace Cody, first daughter of Sara and Joe. (Ellie Mary followed in 2002, much to the joy of all concerned.) Daisy entered the world on July 29, just twenty minutes before the birthday of her great-grandmother, Joan Hodgson. Yet Daisy only had five months to be cuddled by and smile at her beloved grandfather, Geoffrey, before he passed into the world of light very suddenly, on 30 December 1999, when he was little

Geoffrey with Melanie beside him at the 1998 London Lodge Christmas Fair

over sixty. Melanie enjoyed just over a year of marriage to him, and the loss all round was a huge one.

Geoffrey had been living with chronic lymphatic cancer for some time, but his passing into the world of light was unexpected, and occurred just after the festival of Christmas, so that it echoed the shock of the passing of John Hodgson some years earlier. In similar circumstances, the extreme grief of loss was again a learning experience for us all, helping us to realise how close the world of spirit is. Geoffrey's passing led to some wonderful moments of contact. Jeremy wrote in STELLA POLARIS of an experience he had in Geoffrey's office:

Geoffrey Dent

'I think a soul's passing often does shed a radiance into the physical level, and at that visit the office where he worked seemed just full of a radiant peace. I did not hear words, but if I had to put that peace into words it would be that Geoffrey was saying, "It's all okay. You can let go of it all. Everything in life and earth is okay". There was a feeling of radiant philosophical acceptance which was always part of Geoffrey's spirit.'

Others shared similar experiences, of love and reassurance, both from Geoffrey and from the angels of healing. 'It was really a confirmation for me of the truth of White Eagle's words', Geoffrey's daughter, Sara, wrote. 'If you ask for help, and if you can "still the storm" and calm yourself for long enough, the help will come. In my worst moments, I made an enormous effort to calm myself, to tune in and raise my consciousness to the light, and quite honestly I received a miraculous healing. It was as if a blanket had been lifted. I have never experienced anything like it.' Sara was also conscious of Geoffrey's voice saying clearly 'There is nothing to fear' – 'which was very significant to me', she writes, 'as overcoming fear has always been my biggest lesson to learn'.

Geoffrey in fact helped many to overcome fear during his life on the physical plane. He truly devoted his later life to helping others, yet in unobtrusive, practical and realistic ways. He was loved by all the New Lands office staff, where he worked as Treasurer for so many years. Jeremy wrote 'I have been greatly touched by the affection those who worked for or with Geoffrey had for him … people felt safe with him. Many have said how he always brought a feeling of security. I don't believe this was only because he was a skilled accountant and manager of so much of the Lodge's material affairs, I think it was because people knew they were talking to someone who took a particularly full and honest responsibility for his own emotions, and so they felt a corresponding relief and security in his presence'. Even those with whom Geoffrey had dealt at a business level – suppliers and book distributors, for instance – were eloquent about what a good man he was to deal with. Geoffrey's work as Treasurer of the Lodge for so many years combined with his work as a minister, and he was greatly loved for his down-to-earth, witty and enlightening talks in services. After his passing, a member wrote 'I never missed a service when Geoffrey was the speaker; always there was a new, profound slant on the teachings, delivered with humour'. Summing up the feelings of so many, a brother wrote 'When Geoffrey was present; I always felt that all was well'. Jeremy's phrase from the Old Testament at Geoffrey's cremation is eloquent, too: 'an Israelite in whom there was no guile'.

'The cycle of life' was at one time the title of this section. It is a phrase that works in many different ways. In many respects, the 1990s were one of the strongest growth periods in the entire history of the Lodge. Yet Geoffrey would have been the first to speak in terms of an inbreathing and outbreathing in financial affairs. As the millennium closed, it became painfully clear how the funds that had fuelled the period of expansion had simply run out (despite endless attempts to rectify this, the Lodge has always been heavily prone to dependence on the very uneven flow of legacies for its funding). After Geoffrey's passing, he was missed in countless ways, but none more so than for his invaluable work as Treasurer of the White Eagle Lodge, a job which had a huge urgency to it, in view of the precarious situation in which the Lodge found itself. Geoffrey was a difficult act to follow, and we trusted that the brothers in the light had a plan for his successor, just as they had many years before, when Geoffrey ably took over the finances from John Hodgson.

Our faith proved justified when in 2000, Stuart Neil, a brother of the Lodge for many years, stepped into the breach. He was also just the right man to pull us through some horribly stringent years when staff levels had to be reduced, salaries capped, and painful economies made all round. As much tribute should go to those who bore these economies as to anyone who was with us in moments of success. Stuart, who was used to incredibly hard work, had been a young member of the Lodge some forty years previously as an 'Eaglet' (see p. 64) and had since enjoyed a varied and successful career that ranged from banking to running a charity in India, leaving him very well-qualified for the job. STELLA POLARIS reported at the time that 'when we first knew him he had just trained as a banking inspector, so we feel sure that the Lodge accounts are in good hands!'. He has brought a renewed sense of purpose to the work as well as many other blessings, not least his keen sense of humour, another area in which Geoffrey's passing left a large gap to fill!

Stuart Neil

*

Despite the shortage of funds, the year 2000 is actually to be remembered as a year for new design and development. In June 2000 the Garden of Communion that Joan had foreseen, created at the side of the Temple, and looking out to the south and west (the direction that has always offered the best views from New Lands), was opened to all for private meditation and contemplation. The circular paved design is complemented by drifts of hanging roses, and a gentle fountain with water trickling over gleaming rocks and pebbles was positioned in the middle of one circle, next to the carved bench dedicated to Joan and John. Joe Cody's garden design honoured Joan's vision and was of two connected circles, making it a particularly appropriate location to not only remember both Joan and John but also Geoffrey, as the second circle held another seat, under a rose bower, facing a sundial. The unique iron gate holds a central six-pointed star shape through which the garden visitor can look out across the Temple hill to distant woods, while visitors to the Temple can emerge through a side door directly into the garden.

There was also a slightly larger new design to be welcomed in 2000! Celebrations were held in America as the new retreat house was opened at the centre in Texas on 26 March 2000. Jenny performed the special opening ceremony with Jean and the Retreat Home was dedicated to our founders, Minesta and Brother Faithful, in recognition of their ongoing legacy, the worldwide White Eagle work. One might add that in the dedication was also remembered Minesta's often-forgotten talent of homemaker!

Jean later described the new building, 'with white bricks and a forest green roof.... When you enter through exquisite stained glass and oak doors, you see a wide reception area. To the right, graceful, arched alcoves lead to the spacious dining area where gourmet vegetarian meals will be served. Large windows overlook the Temple of the Golden Rose and the grounds. In the sheltered terrace guests can enjoy a magnificent view of the meadow and forest or bask in

Joe takes a break as the Garden of Communion takes shape

Here it is! – so lovely – the Americas Retreat Center

The rest of Joe's family: Sara (centre) is surrounded by brother Michael Dent, mother Jenny, and children Daisy and Ellie

The Lodges in London and at New Lands are proud to host some of the vital meetings of umbrella organisations in the fields of healing, astrology and elsewhere. Here, in the London Lodge, recognition is given, to David Repard, for many years chair of the Confederation of Healing Organisations, on his retirement

the warm healing pool with jet sprays to ease tired muscles and soak away the stress of everyday life. A library, comfortably set out, with fireplace and shelves of books, offers a quiet respite. Perhaps the highlight of the building is the chapel, adorned by the loved stained glass windows. Come and see for yourself. You will be welcomed in the traditional Texas style'. Colum wrote, 'It looks fresh and new, but also as though it has grown up naturally out of the ground.... It has been beautifully designed to make the best use of the site, with glorious views of the surrounding land from every room....'

Jenny described for STELLA POLARIS the service of dedication, in which she paid tribute to the hard work of Jean and John LeFevre, writing 'I still remember being taken to the land in 1986 and experiencing with Jean and John the beauty of the vision we held. Even then we felt the strength and power of the ancient sun brothers and knew it was right for the work and the Star Centre to be established there. Gradually the vision unfolded further and the Temple, and now the Retreat Home, took physical manifestation.'

New design, in 2000, didn't mean just building or garden design, either! A new blueprint for the working practices of healers in Britain was also being developed at this time, with the creation of a new umbrella group 'UK Healers' (UKH), which effectively took over several of the previous roles of the Confederation of Healing Organisations. UKH has evolved into a collaboration between 38 key spiritual healing organisations, and has worked with the Prince of Wales Foundation for Integrated Health. Its work has also been affected by a key House of Lords report on complementary therapies and their regulation. UKH aimed to become the lead body for practising healers in Britain, following assiduously the route of self regulation. Jeremy Hayward, who with Anna had overseen the expansion of our own healing training during the 1990s, gratefully accepted the help of Jan de Vulder, who took on at this time the formal sounding role of 'Contact Healing Training Standards Officer'. Jan has been our representative at UKH meetings ever since and has enabled the Lodge to contribute to the development of a new set of national standards for training and assessment, a fresh national Code of Conduct, and several policies for healing practice. At the time of writing, UKH has succeeded in setting up a structure for accrediting the training programmes of individual organisations, and a landmark moment in the winter of 2008 was the accreditation of the Lodge's newly developed comprehensive training manual for healers. The healing work has always been at the core of the Lodge's purpose and central to White Eagle's teachings; it is also a key way through which we offer service into the wider community. The public standing achieved through public standing enables us to extend this service.

Good news was received at the start of the new millennium from many of our European centres, reporting expansion in various new areas. The White Eagle work gained momentum in Hungary, where the group leader, Bela Balogh, reported: 'We have twenty-six regular members; I hope we will have a good strong base with some good healers in a few years'. STELLA POLARIS echoed: 'It is so good to see this unfoldment of the Brotherhood work in Eastern Europe'. Similarly in Belgium, Marthe Huyghe, leader of the work there, was thrilled at the success of a three-day retreat in an abbey south of Brussels. This was a first for the 'small, but dedicated, family in Belgium', and Marthe wrote that they were 'so grateful for this special opportunity of bringing people together in harmony and joy under the Star'. Building on foundations laid by Hanne Jahr and others, another small but dedicated group of faithful 'Star workers' for the light were also 'keeping on keeping on' in Norway, under the leadership of Ines Vargas. Ines is a dedicated brother who has also inspired and assisted the work of our group in Chile – another case of the light stretching boundlessly between continents!

Sandor from Sweden visits the group in Hungary in 2003

This progress and development was matched in Sweden, where ambitious plans to build a Temple were unveiled. One of the Swedish Star brothers, Torgny Jansson, said in correspondence: 'I think that our new Temple will be very beautiful. We will just have to do it ourselves, because we will have no money to hire any workers.... We think it is much better to build ourselves – it is a different energy. How often in our incarnations do we get an opportunity to build a White Eagle temple? We just can't miss this chance that God has given us'.

Could there be any more encouraging words, to anyone in a similar position? We remember another brother who said, 'I know it is my work in this life to build this Temple, and if I don't I will have failed!'. Well, we don't really believe in failure, but it is the feeling of absolute commitment to the ideal, of a vocation to do something, which perhaps characterises the whole of this story.

The optimism behind the Swedish building proved justified when Jenny dedicated the Temple in 2001. The new designs did not stop there, however, as Sandor and his dedicated helpers then went on to design and create a new garden of communion around the Temple. Jenny wrote that 'There are two lotus pools with goldfish, and also running water in different areas of the garden. In one, there is a white seat of communion and the other is guarded by a white eagle.'

Inspirational vision was reflected in Denmark, as well, where plans were revealed for an extra-special extension to the Polaris centre – a new Temple there too! Grethe wrote in 2001 that they had 'exactly completed the five-year plan which we set out in October 1996, when we bought the Polaris centre.... We are now making the next plan, but this time it is for three years. We can see the building full of joyful people....' Grethe and Rolf described themselves as 'going forward in faith with the new building.... In a miraculous way, money has been given. This expansion of the work is only pos-

THE STORY OF THE WHITE EAGLE LODGE

sible, we know, because of the support, dedication and hard work of all the brothers and sisters of the Danish Lodge'.

The elegant, simple building was completed very soon in true White Eagle style. Jenny led the blessing and dedication of the new building, in a service which drew on the traditions of all our world religions, describing it as 'wonderfully designed and inspiring'. So many of the leaders of other European centres were present at the dedication that Grethe and Rolf felt it was 'like one big family. We thank you for all your support and trust and will continue the work – just keeping on keeping on'.

Some of the ways in which 2000 proved to be a year of new design were quite unexpected. Early in the year, a refurbishment of the Temple Foyer was completed, a project which, like that of the communion garden, had been conceived as a way of commemorating twenty-five years since the Temple's opening. The foyer had been redesigned to give it a warmer feel as a gathering place, and the three original doors from the foyer into the main Temple were replaced with a new triptych, the central panel of which contains a six-pointed Star window in cut glass. Then, at the end of a week which had brought several challenges, on Friday the thirteenth (yes!) of October we were presented with a totally unexpected opportunity to refurbish the Temple interior. A fire which began from a curtain becoming entangled with a spotlight rapidly spread, and within an hour and a half all the interior decoration and furnishings of the main Temple were damaged beyond repair by smoke and charring.

The fire was a traumatic event for those at New Lands, and indeed everyone who knew and loved the Temple in its original state, and left widespread shock. However, it was strongly felt as the weeks passed, that the fire had a spiritual purpose, and was significant at an energetic level. These thoughts were shared in an appeal letter to Members, which spoke of a deep feeling of spiritual cleansing, and a clearing away of old patterns of thought. One Member put it: 'The flames were golden flames of purification. The golden flames were burning up outworn energies … in order to move forward into a deeper, freer place of sunlight'. The letter also spoke of the opportunity to refurbish the Temple to create a home suited to the needs of the new century.

The combination of a wonderfully warm response to the appeal, and the outcome of the insurance claim made, did indeed provide the opportunity for a renewing and refreshing of the building in many ways – and on more than just an outward level. Events worked so that we did not appoint a main contractor, but dealt directly with a wide variety of local contractors and trades; these included friends of the Lodge working in a professional capacity. In fact, a noteworthy feature of the refurbishment as a whole was the extent of community involvement, with greatly appreciated

Morgan (inside the altar) and Peter (on the saffold tower) were just two of our gallant member-helpers after the fire

voluntary contributions playing a part at all stages. We indeed felt thankful to White Eagle's family of Members.

During the closure, the quiet work of healing, and the Brotherhood work, continued as usual, with small and intimate services taking place in the old (and rather nostalgic) setting of New Lands Chapel. The day of reopening, 10 June 2001, was a moment of great joy. We said welcome to the new, more delicate, colours of the interior (amethyst and cream) and the tranquil and lighter effect of the design. Tribute should be paid at this point to the artistry of our professional advisor, Geoffrey Player, a London Member, who worked closely with Jeremy Hayward, as also did Simon Bentley. Long hours were spent establishing the right colour combinations, fabrics, lighting effects and a new altar area. Yes, we felt that out of the trauma had been born something of greater beauty, and a fitting home which would meet the needs of White Eagle's work and its friends for many years to come.

The Temple reopening was also the moment to launch a long-awaited publication, THE LIGHT BRINGER. Here, the book is inspected by Jan de Vulder (New Lands), Ylana, Geoffrey Player and Anna Hayward, the book's primary compiler

*

The refurbished Temple was opened just in time to become the setting for a Summer Festival, and a little later a Family Camp. By 2001, the Family Camp had already become an important and popular annual event at New Lands. The initial vision which led to the camp was one of spiritual community, 'Ohana' in the native American phrase, and the pioneers of the camp, Roslyn Aubrey and Malcolm and Sue White, saw in the setting of the Temple hilltop the opportunity to bring families – with children of all ages – together. The shared life of the camp brought the opportunity for each family to contribute whatever skills and activities it wished to share, and the principle of entertaining ourselves rather than replying on outside stimulus was important from the beginning.

August 2001 brought a test of the camp ideals – and of the canvas of our tipi - as it rained, rained … and rained. In true White Eagle style, however, the rain did not dampen spirits, and the organisers commented that 'there was real feeling of Brotherhood in action'. Jenny, who was very involved in the camp activities wrote that 'many of the children have now come to the camp five years in a row, developing ongoing friendships. Children have become teenagers. The strength of this is to bring into our wide family a very special feeling of a tribe of children growing up together under the Star'. During the camp, the newly reopened Temple was also the setting for a White Eagle Christening for four of the children, at their own request.

Another principle of the camp that has evolved, although it is in every way children-orientated, is that the camp community throws together children of all ages, along with parents and friends – the feeling of 'tribe' is real, and we feel that it is healthy and creative.

Scenes from Family Camps

Kathryn Bingham, who has done so much to make the Family Camp a success

Our ideal is freedom within safety. There is a wealth of different backgrounds, and we have also been able to provide for children with specific needs. While the ongoing aspiration is to offer an experience of 'childhood in the sunlight', camps are now centered round a particular theme such as 'the four elements', 'peoples of the world' as well as 'the magic of animals'. This particular theme, in 2005, brought an especially evocative camp, and just as we had finished our opening ceremony a beautiful flight of geese, their feathers coloured by the rays of the setting sun, flew closely over the circle – an answering response, it truly felt, from the animal kingdom we were seeking to honour. The camp is now co-ordinated by Kathryn Bingham with a supportive team including teenagers and each year brings new activities, experiences, friendships, learning – and, it must be said, a wonderful exhilaration! We sometimes wish that all Members could come as flies on the wall at the concluding talent show!

The camps have brought new direction to the White Eagle work for families and children – started so many years previously by Joan Hodgson – as a whole, and as well as a regular newsletter and monthly activities we believe that out of this community experience will come materials which we can publish, offering what we have learnt to families both within the White Eagle work and outside.

*

The work in West Africa also continued to flourish in 2002, with a wonderful effort being made at a distance by the London-based brothers we have already mentioned, Frederick and Hamida, who between them devoted a large proportion of their time to coordinating the work in West Africa and visiting the growing number of groups and members there (We have already shown a selection of photographs, all together, on page 130.) They visited groups all over Nigeria and led a brotherhood retreat in Eastern Nigeria, reporting that 'if the love, joy and enthusiasm evident during the eight days were anything to go by, then Eastern Nigeria is off to a bright 'Starlit' start'.

Their visit to Nigeria was followed by a visit to Ghana by Frederick, where he met the Accra group leader Evelyn Addy, daughter of Robert, and was enormously impressed by her commitment and effort in the work. He watched as Evelyn took part in a radio programme and answered questions with a 'simplicity of approach, good delivery, good humour and knack of making difficult topics understandable' that 'won her many fans'. Frederick wrote that 'the Light is reaching many hearts. Many are responding to the stimulation of the light in the heart. The lone worker or few dedicated groups are acting as lighthouses of the soul to their communities'. This moving summary of the progression of the work in Africa reflected the contribution made by so many people in many countries, who have donated White Eagle books or materials to be given to West African members who are unable to purchase them.

Otherwise, 2002 started with Jenny revisiting South Africa, where she became very aware of the importance of the healing of Africa as 'crucial to the healing of the whole world'. STELLA POLARIS commented that 'deep lessons of true brotherhood are being learned. Maybe the rest of the world has to learn from Africa's capacity for happiness, apparent so many times in the midst of its suffering'. During her visit, Jenny visited groups in Durban and Cape Town, spending time with the South African leader, Maybelle van Warmelo, and wrote that she was 'immediately struck how the spiritual power has increased in the four years since my previous visit. The light is strong and vibrant here and a centre for the Brotherhood is being established'. The truth of this statement was shown when, just two years after Jenny's visit, the Cape Town group left their home of the past thirteen years and moved into a new one, much better situated – the loft of a town house with views of Table Mountain. Maybelle wrote that 'we now have a simple, light sanctuary with pine floors and a view over the rooftops to our beacon, Table Mountain. It's easy to see the Star shining out over it!'

Cape Town group today

During her 2002 visit, Jenny spent time with Evelyn van Vloten, the Durban group leader. It was a particularly memorable visit for Jenny, made more so by Evelyn's passing into the world of light shortly afterwards. Evelyn (the right hand figure in the trio in the picture) had been one of the original 'Eaglets' in England in the 1950s and 1960s before moving to spread the light in South Africa, where she led the White Eagle work in Natal for many years. We have also paid tribute (p. 83) to the way in which Evelyn nursed Minesta. Ylana wrote at the time of Evelyn's passing that 'it is lovely to think of her free and happy in her new life, to which she was welcomed with great love'. Jenny wrote feelingly that 'Evelyn brought great fun into my life and whenever I have met her, the same has been true – always this wonderful ray of sunshine, fun and happiness'.

Maybelle, Evelyn, Evelyn: symbols of the work in Africa

*

London was also much affected by physical loss at this time. In many ways, although Colum, as Minister in residence, kept his presence very strongly there even after beginning a private venture, 'Polair Publishing', in September 2003 (it continues to offer a window for White Eagle authors and others, trade conditions permitting), the most visible of the brothers beside Colum throughout the 1990s had been Michael Collishaw ('Michel'), who is already part of this story, Anne Cornock-Taylor ('Diana') and Monique Regester ('White Rose'). By the end of April 2005 all three had left their physical bodies.

The first to pass on was Anne, on 30 January 2000. Anne was one

Anne Cornock-Taylor, 1950s

Monique Regester, in a later picture, stands before Christmas flowers she herself arranged

of a small group of friends within the work who had met through Margaret Morris Movement, a dance technique which began in Glasgow; although it was the Principal of the London School, Betty Simpson, who was the major link between them. Anne was a handsome woman with a remarkable carriage as well as the most loving, twinkling eyes, and as her contact deepened she was also a remarkable mentor to many within the work, a responsibility she handled with the professionalism of a counsellor. She was a painter, too, and her paintings were one of the mainstays of the 1994 art exhibition (see p. 122). In later years she brought a wonderful sense of continuity to the work, having come to it in the 1940s and been initiated in 1948. She knew exactly how tradition worked for best and worst and, without the slightest sense of narrowed focus, she set the highest standards for herself. She was yet another of our wonderful flower-arrangers, for artistically those standards were never a restriction, simply a fine discipline. And this same concern for standards showed in Anne as cancer finally took over her body: there can be few who better demonstrated their absolute understanding of White Eagle's teaching on their deathbed. Her eyes never shone so much as they did there, as though full of the glory of spirit.

In the latter part of her life, her closest friend and companion was Monique Regester. Monique came not from 'MMM' but from France, via the White Eagle group in Saffron Walden, Essex. This was led by Eileen and Alan Thompson, a couple whose Quaker roots always showed strongly in their loving devotion to the work of the inner light (Alan is to be seen in the picture top left on p. 100, and Eileen in the work week picture on p. 71). They were the perfect bridge between Monique's inherited French Catholicism and the open understanding and freedom of thought within the White Eagle work, and when Monique's marriage foundered she came to London to stay with Anne … and never left.

Monique was a true artist, but in the context of a craftsperson above all. Her particular speciality was crêpe paper and wax flower-arrangements, a craft in which she was possibly the sole survivor of an old tradition. She knew perfectly how to arrange flowers, too, like Anne – so that the London Lodge, when Anne and Monique had done the flowers, was a perfect temple to the beauty in nature. Monique also very much took on the role of mother-figure in the London Lodge, before and after Anne's passing. She trained many 'daughters' along the path and was loved by all. Her health, always a little precarious, finally failed her and she passed over on 31 March 2003. Eileen, by the way, who had brought her into the work and was a tireless volunteer at New Lands (particularly at garden parties, when younger), passed on a year later, in 2004, though her husband Alan is still with us, one of our lively nonagenarians.

Yet not content with losing two of its best servants, the London

Lodge was due to lose yet another of its pillars – one who was a pillar of the work worldwide too. On 14 April 2005, Michael Collishaw, Brother Michel, left his physical body after an illness that had removed him from active work a full eighteen months before. He had been a most valued Trustee of the Lodge (ultimately as Chair) for many years and also worked tirelessly for the American and Dutch Lodges, but beyond this he represented one of the Lodge's richest links with its past, as a compassionate and sociable being who knew a great many people in the Lodge, often deeply, and he had a very good memory too. He kept intimacies close to his heart, and gave forth his opinions only when called upon to do so, but when he did he rarely offered less than real wisdom. He truly upheld the dignity of the work, and gave the impression of having been involved with it always. In fact, he had been initiated back in 1953 after coming to the Lodge at the side of his mother Ann some years before, and maybe the greatest mark of his service had been the way in which he created the White Eagle youth, social and working-party group, the 'Eaglets', described on page 64, and also allowed it to close when Minesta, acting on her guidance from spirit, said that it should continue no longer.

Many were the White Eagle children to whom he was a loving godfather, both in an appointed role and by virtue of the wise interest he took in them. The whole work misses Michael today, and not least the London Lodge.

Tributes to Michael poured in. Jean LeFevre wrote of his passing

Monique takes a healing service – in the Brotherhood Chapel of the old London Lodge…

THE STORY OF THE WHITE EAGLE LODGE

...while Michael leads an Absent Healing Group, in the chapel next door

in terms that would make him a near-perfect example for a Brother of the Lodge. 'During the forty-five years I have known him, Michael rarely criticised and preferred to remain in the background. His knowledge of the White Eagle teachings was outstanding and his small personal chapel was a place of peace and serenity. He suffered his illness with great fortitude and no complaints, believing in God's will.' Michael was especially well loved for his invaluable work with groups in the Netherlands, where he frequently travelled to lead retreats. In what seemed a fitting tribute to him, the new Star Centre of the South Netherlands was dedicated in a beautiful retreat weekend that was attended by many European leaders. In the Centre Pages of STELLA POLARIS it was pointed out that 'it seemed very special that this new birth for the work in the Netherlands should take place just after Michael Collishaw's passing. Many felt that Michael was present throughout the proceedings in his shining body of light'. Tribute was paid to him in the dedication service by Stuart Neil, the new Lodge treasurer, one of Michael's many lifelong friends.

Meanwhile, our love and congratulation to those who try to fill the places left by Anne, Monique and Michael: Esme and John, Kath, Colin, Joan and Susan, Richard, Brown and Hazel, and all the rest.

CHAPTER VIII

Uniting under the Star: Renewed Vision

A REGIONAL Centres Conference took place at New Lands in May 2006. Described by participants as an 'inspiring gathering', the conference brought together about thirty regional leaders from around the UK and those working at New Lands and the London Lodge. The aim was to give practical form to a vision for youw members of White Eagle's family countrywide could best be offered support and oportunities for involvement. As a result of the conference a new structure was developed, with the UK divided into fourteen geographical regions. Each region would have one or two co-ordinators, helped by a supporting team of brothers who would be responsible for special regional events including open days, and for networking within the region generally. Those taking on this work do so on an entirely voluntary basis, and like Daughter Lodge leaders are making a most wonderful contribution to nurturing and supporting White Eagle's family.

An earlier meeting in 1998, when overseas leaders met Mother Lodge Ministers and Trustees

As early as 2004, Jenny had felt moved to share a vision and plan for regional centres which had crystallised under White Eagle's inspiration. Now, giving a talk on 'earthing the Master's vision', Jenny said: 'Our new vision of different UK regions together encompassing the whole of the UK means that eventually every single member and friend in the UK will have both a first and a second point of contact – the Mother Lodge at New Lands and their own regional centre. We feel sure that everyone can appreciate the benefits of this. The Lodge as a whole can provide much more support and localised service to its members and the regional centre is instrumental in achieving this to a much greater extent than is possible for many groups.'

In many ways the pioneer White Eagle regional centre was that for the South West of England. The South West centre did not develop around an existing daughter Lodge and its building, but showed that it was possible to hold all kinds of regional meetings – from open days to Brotherhood Meetings – at hired venues such as village halls and guide huts. In this way members and brothers from the extreme South West of Cornwall through to Somerset could become strongly involved, and all 'own' their regional centre. We would like to pay special tribute to Josephine and David Edge

Jo & David Edge

who brought wonderful warm networking skills to their pioneer co-ordinating role, and also showed it was possible for a regional centre in effect to have a portable chapel or chapels! Jo and David shared some of their experience at the conference in May 2006, and at the time of writing the most recent regional centre to be dedicated is that for Wales, where we feel there is a Celtic heritage resonating strongly with White Eagle's work. The new model of regional centres has subtly changed the character of the organisation, and brought a feeling of 'we are one family together', replacing a pyramidal structure.

The increased communication within White Eagle's family was not confined to the UK, however. The internet was allowing greater and easier links between members all the time, something that distinctly increased at the launch of a new website in 2006. The existing website, whose creation in 1998 we mentioned on p. 109, had a splendid overhaul, making the site even more accessible for members. The new one was developed through a great deal of effort put in by Lodge brother Bob Bain, working alongside the multitalented Anna Hayward.

Another conference bringing together worldwide leaders took place in 2004 in the United States at the Temple of the Golden Rose, the first-ever international group leaders' gathering to be held outside the UK. Leaders from Britain, Australia and America created what was described as a 'historic linking-up of the triangle of the three temples'. They were joined by leaders from Sweden, Norway, Switzerland, Germany, South Africa, Mexico and Canada, in a gathering that truly emphasised the new worldwide scale of White Eagle's work, and enabled the different countries to build on the inner closeness and unity of purpose that draws White Eagle's family together. A participant described it as 'a time of learning and sharing on many levels, giving us many opportunities to learn about White Eagle's work in centres all over the world. Perhaps the most moving moment was during Jenny's closing talk, when it was as though we listened to the voice of our beloved teacher White Eagle himself: so vibrant, so strong, telling us all to plough our furrows straight with our eyes ever on the Star, and to serve the light with love for all humankind in our hearts.

'These were very special days, not easily to be forgotten. It is very difficult to convey in a few short words what took place. All those at St John's worked so very hard and with such love for the success of this occasion'.

A strong presence at the conference was Jane Sorbi. She and her husband Jack, both of whom had been involved in the work for many years, had by this time retired from earthly employment and had moved to Texas in 1995 entirely to devote themselves to the work. Jane was ordained as a Minister of the White Eagle Lodge

Jane Sorbi is seen here with Denise Badmington, another key worker at the Texas Center

on 21 February 2005 alongside Simon Bentley, whose commitment and devotion had also qualified him for this most beautiful Brotherhood ceremony.

As we close the period of research for this book, Astra Ferro (in charge of the Absent Healing department, as well as Personnel Officer) has just made the second of two very successful visits to Japan, where there is tremendous interest in White Eagle's work; and Jenny has just visited equally enthusiastic groups of enquirers and members in Hungary.

*

To celebrate the seventieth anniversary of the White Eagle work in 2006, a rather beautiful idea was given to a brother of the Lodge: to donate seventy books and send them out from each of the three Temples, with a label inside asking whoever finds them to read them and pass them on, or leave them in some other public place, so that others may find the books and enjoy them. Our brother wrote: 'Like the people we come to love and who win our hearts, the White Eagle philosophy can find us in the strangest ways. Our intention is to let the light of White Eagle's teachings flow into the world as a gift to those searching for a more beautiful version of life and living. Part of the vision is that the books will provide a way of reaching out across time and space to friends and strangers, and possibly provide just the remedy to the hearts of people searching for greater comfort, love and happiness in their lives. It is envisaged the copies will travel across the world, spreading Star Light as they go!'

Doris Commins and daughter Gay Robinson

The continued importance of the White Eagle publications to the worldwide work was again emphasised when, during the Brotherhood Retreat Morning on 11 June, one copy of every White Eagle book and CD was blessed as a symbol of the wider blessing on all our publications as they go out into the world (one copy of each new publication has in fact always been left on New Lands altar after first being issued). In the words of White Eagle: 'Every printed word which goes forth from this Lodge is to be held in the Star, this is a sacred trust. See that the word of truth and love and goodwill and wisdom goes forth over the whole earth from this Brotherhood.'

The message that went with them is one that provides an appropriate summary or conclusion to this story. The story so far, anyway... The story of our *first* seventy years.

Yet our subtitle is 'seventy-five years of work with the light'. If we return for the moment to the start of this book, it is quickly revealed that it begins with the start of the Brotherhood work in 1934 (or with Burstow, in 1932, or with the initiation of Minesta and Brother Faithful in 1931 – you can choose your date!). Clearly, the moment of beginning is rather arbitrary; but seventy-five years

The circle on the lawn at the 2008 conference both symbolises the atmosphere and indicates the amount of sunshine we enjoyed!

John LeFevre (see p.152)

seems a better way of expressing the length of time we have been working than an exact seventy-two, based on February 22, 1936. The reason for mentioning this now, though, is that the longer date contains a reminder that the work is primarily a brotherhood, and only secondly an organisation.

Rarely has this brotherhood connection between us been more prominently brought to the fore than at the very final event that printer deadlines allow us to cover. At the time of Minesta's birthday in 2008 – in fact from 6 to 12 June – the three Mothers of the brotherhood work, all the leaders of Star centres round the world (bar three, prevented by ill-health), and including all the Ministers of the work, have been together in conference yet again. Not in a formal way, as in an organisation or business, but simply as brothers, one to another. The occasion has felt almost as it must have done when the little band of brothers met together at the beginning of the work, except that now each participant has represented many, many, more besides themselves. The occasion has seen the true birth of our new Wisdom School, which Jenny mentions shortly, at 10 am on 9 June, at a special ceremony. It has seen the results of our recent strategic review put before the leaders from round the world. It has seen the planting of a crystal on Temple Hill, and the rededication of the silver Star we use for our work at the Mother Lodge from its Polaire original. That in particular seems most appropriate at a time of new beginning, which this book celebrates. Above all, we have shared our love with one another, and shall continue to do so for a long time yet.

*

In Native American culture, the Grandmother of the tribe is a figure of experience and wisdom that guides and advises the leaders of a tribe. As the seventieth anniversary of the White Eagle work drew nearer, the Lodge Mother, Ylana Hayward, took the decision to step back from the day-to-day rigours of the role. Ylana, with her co-Lodge Mother Joan Hodgson, had led the Lodge since 1979, and guidance from spirit now led her to make the decision to guide the future growth of the work as Spiritual Grandmother, her work becoming advisory and inspirational. This symbolic act itself gives new meaning to leadership within the work.

After a life spent in training in White Eagle's service, Jenny Dent thus became the Mother of the Lodge in 2005. 'I am so grateful for the help and training I have received over the years for this role', Jenny said. 'My work really began when I worked closely with my grandmother, Grace Cooke, in preparing the manuscript for the book the illumined ones when I was eighteen. Over the years since then, I have worked side by side with my mother Joan and aunt Ylana, and I am honoured to continue to serve under the Star as Mother of the Lodge. It is wonderful that I can do so with the continued physical guidance of Ylana, as well as the spiritual guidance from White Eagle and those in spirit.'

In the Americas, Jean LeFevre has watched Ylana's move with interest and she, too, has taken on the role of Spiritual Grandmother. The Mother of the work in the Americas is now Jane Sorbi, who for many years (from 1983, in fact) was a skilled and much-loved co-ordinator and correspondent for the White Eagle healing – and a group leader in Raleigh, North Carolina, before she and her husband Jack moved to Texas. The work in the Americas also has a new Treasurer, Kathy Evans, since upon reaching his 90th birthday the redoubtable John LeFevre retired (see p. 150). As we go to press, the news has just come through of his transition to spirit, and we think of him going forward into the light, a true soldier of the light indeed. Our love in great measure goes to Jean.

At the ceremony in Texas

The progress from a single Mother of the work, such as Minesta, to one in which the whole work has both an active Mother and a wise Grandmother, is a milestone. It heralds another new phase in the living, growing White Eagle work, and it recognises the way in which (as White Eagle has told us), leadership is a job like any other in the Brotherhood. Today, across the world there are three Mothers and two Grandmothers, each with their own qualities and together sharing a vision; a vision of Brotherhood and love, a vision that was first expressed by Minesta more than seventy years previously. The united family that the White Eagle Lodge has brought into being – a family that extends worldwide and into the realms of spirit – moves forward now, led by Jenny and Ylana; united in Brotherhood, and under the Star.

Ylana on her eighty-seventh birthday

Looking Back; Looking Forward

Jenny Dent writes:

RE-READING the entire manuscript of this book has been a deeply moving experience for me. It records the highs and lows of the history of the Lodge, the service and subsequent passing of some of my own close family members and others very dear to me, and the extraordinary dedication of so many who have given their hearts and their lives to this work.

THE WHITE EAGLE LODGE STORY is a story about people – their courage, their heartaches, their triumphs and their challenges, but above all their faith and ability to 'keep on keeping on' no matter what. The people are the pillars of this work, the pillars of the three physical temples – the light of which shines across the world, linking all White Eagle Centres, all members, all whose hearts have been touched by the magic of the Star.

The very building of these temples was not without struggle and challenge, as this story records. To those who question, 'Surely White Eagle should have smoothed the way when the work was so important?', the answer seems to be both the greater the importance of the work, the greater the testing of those involved in its creation, and also the fact that it is only through the fine-tuning of our individual faith, courage and persistence that the truly strong and enduring foundations are laid. We read in the early chapters of the original edition of how almost immediately after the bombing of our first Lodge in London, Minesta set out to look for another building, and that 'as far as Minesta was concerned, the greater the catastrophe, the greater the courage'.

In my own memory, there was a time in January 1973 when all seemed to have come to a halt with the building of the New Lands Temple. The builders had gone bankrupt, the site was desolate with two and a half pillars standing forlornly in the bleak winter sunshine, and Brother Faithful was in hospital after a car accident. Pushing my eight-month-old baby, Sara, in her pram around the Temple hilltop, I wondered: 'Why, why, why?' I know now that all of us who have been involved in the building and creation of Star Centres around the world have experienced moments of deep soul-searching. Our faith has been tested and tested, and yet somehow we have managed to do as White Eagle asked and keep on keeping on.

The results can be seen now in our 'golden chain of brotherhood around the world', which is not about buildings, as I am quoted as saying in the main text – it is about people, their hard work, their courage, their love and their faith. Now, as Lodge Mother, and looking to the future of our work, I am so thankful for the firm foundation on which we are building, the foundation of courage, love, faith and of 'keeping on keeping on'. I am thankful for the darker moments, which have made these foundations so firm.

As I write this (in March 2008) we have just completed a year-long strategic review which has involved consulting over eighty of our key workers throughout the United Kingdom. This has been a demanding but truly inspiring process, as we have drawn together into a coherent and clearly-budgeted 'plan of action' our vision for the continued unfoldment of our beautiful work. Although this plan is UK-based, we will be sharing it with our Overseas Centres leaders during our Conference in early June. We shall all take it forward together.

Last year (January–December 2007) was named as our 'Year of Outer Communication and Inner Communion', during which we endeavoured to strengthen all our outer links with our worldwide family of members and brothers. Our magazine *Stella Polaris* had a completely new look, with full colour and a more 'international flavour' as it became truly our members' magazine and part of the UK membership subscription. (Colum masterminded the new design which has received much favourable comment.)

I believe, however, that even more significant than the increased *outer communication* has been the unfoldment of a deeper level of *inner communion* which has affected the whole of our work and lifted it onto a new level. As we built on the first seventy years of establishing the worldwide Lodge work and started out on the next phase, it was and is as though we are on a new spiral, working in a new dimension of understanding and communion. Our whole world is a very different place in this twenty-first century, and so many more people are ready and waiting for the special beauty of White Eagle's teaching and the magic of the Star.

White Eagle himself is now leading us to a greater understanding of his own role. He has never made claims for himself. He has only ever said that he is a spokesperson for a group of illumined souls who work for the upliftment of all life on our planet. After Minesta's passing, he continued to make it very clear that his guidance for our work and the unfolding service of the Star Brotherhood was as strong and powerful as ever. This has become increasingly so, as every year has passed. He does not wish our perception of him to be confined to the native American Indian chief, or the guide of one individual soul. His work is to inspire thousands of souls and I feel that he has had lives in all the world's major religious traditions. This brings a unique flavour to his teaching with so many different interwoven threads. In our current White Eagle Publishing Trust strategy document, one of our stated strategic aims is: 'To let White Eagle stand forth as a wise, venerated spiritual teacher for the modern day, with a practical philosophy for the twenty-first century, which brings together threads from all the world's religions. This teaching is the foundation of the unfolding White Eagle Wisdom School, which will be a 'living school of the spirit'. The 'wisdom school' is fundamental part of our vision and it will embrace many new areas, including further development of our meditation teaching, music, dance and all the creative arts.

However, we will never overlook the fact that a primary aspect of White Eagle's work has always been to help build the bridge between the worlds and alleviate fear of death. He will always seek to help those in incarnation in the physical life make their own clear contact with the heavenly state of being. He has gradually led us away from the traditional idea of a medium channelling a guide's message, to an understanding that all souls have the potential and opportunity for making their own contact and receiving heavenly guidance and inspiration. Minesta and Brother Faithful, Joan and John and other key workers who are now still active in the inner world have truly helped all White Eagle's family in the building of the bridge by which we may cross into that world at will, normally in meditation. The Star wonderfully symbolises the coming together of the two worlds in its interlinked triangles, and it is through the Star that all who love his work and teaching can most easily contact White Eagle.

It is because of the dedication of 'Star workers' for so many years that it has been possible for the illumined teachers for whom White Eagle works to draw closer to earth. The one on the 'John ray', known as 'the Master of the Star', is very much a master of this new age of Aquarius, and White Eagle is his disciple, bringing his–her energy closer to earth through the work of the Star and the service of the Star Brotherhood. This service has unfolded and developed greatly in the last twenty years.

It is really important to note here, too, that White Eagle's work is not dependent on one physical channel. We believe his inspiration will go on through many decades. For the day-to-day guidance of his work he normally uses the one given the role of 'Lodge Mother', but he closely inspires all dedicated White Eagle leaders around the world, thus enabling the work to unfold and develop in the best possible way according to local and cultural conditions, while retaining the same pure golden thread of absolute dedication to the Star.

This golden thread unites us all and leads me to the image of the golden triangle of light between our three Temples. At the beginning of this year (2008), which we have called the Year of our Worldwide Family, White Eagle said to us that he wants all his workers around the world to hold this image, and realise how the golden light of heavenly nourishment and abundance flows around the triangle. This brings all the help and support needed to take the work forward in every country of the world, for all Centres, all brothers, all members, are linked in this golden triangle.

So we look forward into the future with confidence in our ever-unfolding work, with thankfulness for all who have given so much in the past, and are indeed the 'spiritual pillars' or our work, and above all to White Eagle for all his ongoing guidance, inspiration and encouragement.

Looking to the future?

Additional Notes on the Illustrations

6   Minesta (Grace Cooke) as a young woman
8   A detail from the portrait of White Eagle by R. Vicaji
9   Ivan Cooke (Brother Faithful), early 1940s
10   Opening of Burstow, 25 March 1933
11   Fireplace at Burstow Manor   12   Burstow Manor
14   The *Bulletin des Polaires* ran from May 1930 and became *Les Cahiers* in 1933; Minesta at Burstow with Mauris (Anne Bowen), initiated 1935
15   Three of the brothers initiated in 1934: Blue Star (Mrs C. Malcolm); Christian (Ylana Hayward); Ray (Lady Doris Segrave)
16   Burstow Altar; Mary Yoxall's companion Peggy Orr is still with us today
17   Main Chapel, Pembroke Hall
18   Brotherhood Chapel, Pembroke Hall   19   Members' Room, Pembroke Hall
20   White Eagle's Room, Pembroke Hall
21   The duplicated first issue of ANGELUS (bound too tight to avoid distortion)
22   The first major collection of White Eagle's teaching, ILLUMINATION; Johannes (John Hodgson) and Brother Steadfast (Leonard Willis)
23   Reginald Botcherby (Brother John); David Burn-Callander (David)
24   Margaret (Margot) Stedman ('Pearl')
25   Pen-and-ink drawing by Selwyn Dunn (Haslemere, Surrey)
26   Pembroke Hall altar, with lilies. A famous photo was said to show fairies
27   Christmas Tree in Pembroke Hall, 1938
28   Title page of the first printed ANGELUS; Main Chapel and Healing Chapel at 48 Hanover Street, Edinburgh. The chairs are still in use, at New Lands
29   The 'Cross of Light' poster. The 'Underground' picture is iconic of the War
31   At Grubb's Farm, near Biggin Hill in Kent – the unexpected place of sanctuary that saved the lives of Minesta and family
32   The School of Animal Painting for which 9 St Mary Abbots Place had been built just before the First World War. Another shows a class upstairs
33   Letter announcing the new premises and reopening
34   A glimpse of the main chapel shortly after the opening
35   Entrance to 9 St Mary Abbots Place, probably just after the War
36   Joan with daughter Rosemary, born in June 1945
37   Sara Burdett; the footnote suggests how influential she may have been
38   Alison Innes, Sister Pearl; THE CHRISTIAN MYSTERIES, second edition, 1943
39   Bill Patterson holding his daughter Anne. For his wife Nancie, see p. 97
40   Sister Radiant (Kathleen Fleming), one of the Glasgow Lodge pioneers
41   Minesta in the woods near Headley Down; Rake Village, a postcard
42   Aerial photo of New Lands, taken in or before 1956
43   The original altar in New Lands, set up for a christening, maybe Ylana's twins
45   The 1948 Trust Deed, which dealt with London only; Olive Robinson
46   Looking back from the altar, New Jersey chapel; Joan, around 1948
47   A White Eagle wedding in Edinburgh: Mary ('Laughing Water') & Alan Hershey, February 1952; Frank & Bee Wharhirst
48   Family Hodgson: Jenny, John, Rosemary, Joan. At New Lands, as is the next
49   Family Hayward: Geofffrey and Ylana, with Jeremy and Colum
50–   EARLY YEARS AT NEW LANDS : A CELEBRATION
 51   Left-hand page: retreat 1949; retreat 1949; retreat, slightly later; retreat, slightly later; retreat, 1956; retreat, date unknown. Right-hand page: ornamental 'toadstool' in New Lands garden, where there is now a road; the Monks' Walk before the Temple drive was built; New Lands with awning over the chapel window; Joan opens 1956 Garden Party; Ylana leads camp fire singing, possibly same date
 52   Beeches in Monks' Walk, New Lands. The first painting may be late 1940s
 53   Main chapel, London Lodge; Minesta returns to Lordat

54 Michael Collishaw ('Michel'), around 1950; Edna Taylor ('Sunray') as 'land girl', before she came to the Lodge

55 The choir leads out of the London Lodge at the twenty-first birthday service. Ylana conducts; among the men are visible Michael Collishaw and Sir Ronald Fraser ('Nobleheart'), wife of Ingrid Lind ('Silver Star'). Below, Heather Taylor ('Jewel') serves at the party; to the right side of the person being served is Trudi Keller ('Truth') and on her left, Mary Brace

56 Minesta and Brother Faithful cut the cake, same occasion

57 Title page of MORNING LIGHT (1957) and covers of THE RETURN OF ARTHUR CONAN DOYLE and MEDITATION (1955)

59 Christmas Fair, London, 1962: Kathy Green behind the stall. Damaged

60 Minesta and Brother Faithful with Rosemary and Paul Beard ('Truth' and 'Mark'). They holidayed together in the Swiss Alps and the Pyrenees

61 Lit lamp. The floating wick is much loved in the Lodge

62 SPIRITUAL UNFOLDMENT 1 (1961). An expanded edition was published in 2000

63 Gwyn Mennay, the Plymouth Lodge and 'Mary' and 'John' Elliot

64 'Peter' Hamilton; 'Radiance' (Irene Hancock) and 'Peace' (Enid Brown)

65 37 Pompstationsweg, Den Haag: the Dutch Lodge 1965

66 Opening of the Dutch Lodge, with its leader, Margaret Petri-Moora ('Silver Star'), seated right; founders of the Reading Lodge, Betty Jones (also 'Silver Star' and Leonard Lane ('Leo')

69 Rose Elliot (1967)   70 THE QUIET MIND, original edition

71 Work week round New Lands dining room table, 1970s or 1980s; Ellie and Basil Gillam, founders of the first Sydney Daughter Lodge

72– UK DAUGHTER LODGE ROUND-UP. Early picture of Inverleith
73 Row, Edinburgh Lodge; Reading and Worthing Lodges; Crowborough Group (later Daughter Lodge), 1975; Ipswich Lodge in 1995

75 Four shots of the construction of the Temple at New Lands

76 Anthony Elliot and Martin Muncaster, at the Temple opening, 1974

77 Minesta and Brother Faithful lead out, at the opening, 1974

78–9 Temple interior, facing East and West, just after it opened

80 Early activities in the Brisbane Daughter Lodge; stall at Norwegian New Age Festival, date unknown (but substantially later)

81 Sponsored walk (here, across watermeadows near Amberley in Sussex); Accra Group, retreat at New Lands just after 1974

82 Plaque, 'Les Polaires à Brighteyes', given to her some time in the early 1930s

86 The New Lands Temple before it was extended

88 The office extension to New Lands, some works remaining

89 Wendy Collett in her office; the Temple extension grows

90 Australia: the chapel in the wooden cabin; a game outside; the shack Brother Faithful converted, near Harvey, W. Australia, in 1923

91 Colorado Conference 1984, Jenny and Geoffrey below; others better identified in the Long Beach retreat photo, 1985. Back row: Mark Sebastian, John and Jean LeFevre, Hazel Weathers, Alex Cline, Beverley Wyatt. Middle: Mary Hershey, Doris Hagermann, Anne Stine, Kärin Baltzell. Front: Philip Ross, Diane Pomerance, Terri Rosenthal, Craig Syverson, 'Lawrence' Paller

92 Trustees and Daughter Lodge leaders, 1983: Betty Jones (Reading), Dorothy Wright and Joanne Atterbury (Teignmouth); Doris Cooper and Agnes Shellens (Plymouth); Joan, Ylana, Eunice Dixon (Bournemouth), Beryl Waters (Ipswich). Back row: Leo Lane (Reading); Ranald Godfrey (Edinburgh, later Trustee); Jeremy, John, Jenny, Radiance, Noel Gabriel (Trustees), John Kemp (Ipswich); Geoffrey Dent

93 Table in Brotherhood Library designed by Jon Barnsley

94 View along the front of the Temple extension and…

95 …along the New Lands extension

96-7 MEMBERS AND FRIENDS. Top row: John Kemp, Jim and Norah

Ackroyd, Jim Hendren, Nancie Patterson, 'Iona' (Estella McKean), Vera Beck. Middle: Joanne Atterbury (at 100!), Alf Commins, 'Dawn' Chambers, Betty Simpson, Mary Gould, June Billingham, Tony & Marie Bennett, Estelle Stead (in old age). Front: Irene Hume (June) & Eunice Dixon (Dixie) (Bournemouth), 'Nada' (Lily Strode), Ilabelle Shanahan, Dee Morison, 'Lawrence', Edith and Walter Ohr, Nigel Millross

98   Ylana, Joan and John at Golden Jubilee in London; Philip Jones (Brother David) at the Temple organ

99   Golden Jubilee concert; Simon Bentley (Brother Christopher)

100 Top left: Alan Thompson faces camera at left. In the other group, Cynthia Evanson talks to Dorrie Lyon, with Mary Robinson and Heather Agnew behind. Top right: Nancie Downing talks to Jed Clarke and Alex Ross. Centre: Mike Sage, who organised the walk, is left front. Bottom right: Kath and Andy Noctor catch up Geneita Perkins, from Australia

101 'Keep on keeping on' (KOKO): the great White Eagle motto!

102 Gay Robinson as Gay Commins; Lyn Edwards as Lyn Commins

103 Rose Chapel among the pines in Texas, and a work party

104 Sandor and Michel Huszár busy on construction; Doris Commins

105 Concrete slabs poured and set for the Australasian Temple; New York group in 1989 with Karol Reiner, leader, centre; French retreat taken by Colum Hayward and Monique Regester at Plailly-sur-Oise

106 Tipi, Indian Paintbrush, Texas   107 Australasian Temple opening

108 Leeds Lodge, opened in 1988: Joan and John with Bettine Pickles; three editions of Joan's WISDOM IN THE STARS

109 Launch of YOGA OF THE HEART in the Temple: Geoffrey Dent and Jenny Beeken. Cover by much-missed Andrew Slocock (d. 2000)

110 Alison with Colum, Jeremy, Rose, Jenny; Radiance at Burstow in 1960 (Ylana made another pilgrimage in October 2005 with Nigel Millross, Catherine Hamilton, Morgan Hesmondhalgh and Colum)

111 Noel and Loveday Gabriel. Noel was married first to Mary ('Mary'), and then to Loveday ('Christine') shown in the photo, both supportive brothers of the Lodge

112 Anna and Jeremy, singing along at a Garden Party in the early 1990s

113 Golden Mountain model made by Nigel Millross which was intended to be a beacon like the 'lighthouse' of the Million Penny Fund

114 The old London Lodge before refurbishment; loveliest of all was the cranberry lamp on the main altar as all the lights were extinguished. Below, the tea pourers include stalwarts Geoffrey Dent and Wendy Collett and another old friend, 'the Lodge Volvo' (1990s)

115 Mark Leslie's design worked on motifs of circles and semi-circles; they inspired the altar alcoves after the 1995 refurbishment. Mark's father, Desmond ('Aton') was one of the great characters among our brothers and in public view as well, a pioneering researcher of UFOs

116 Heart of England walk, organised by David and Jo Edge (pictured); Retreat Centre nears completion in Australia

117 The trailer was acquired from Belle Lawter, one of the early US brothers, who 'came home' to live there late in life; Michael Collishaw in the 1990s

118 Getting the Americas Temple ready: Colum and David were only two of a huge party of helpers. Below, the bronze entrance doors

119 Everyone is there at the Americas Temple opening! Eric and Shirley Warrington have celebrated many more years of service since 1995....

120 A lovely turnout for the launch of the 1993 Swiss centre, pictured beneath

121 Meeting in the Netherlands; Patricia Fletcher ('Clare'), seen with David and Betty Smith, moved from South Africa to help at New Lands but served as an invaluable link between the two places until Jenny was able to go out. Jenny has revisited Table Mountain twice since 1994

122 The centre in Lagos was run by Regina Olajolo, but the focus has moved

on. In the Cinderella pictures, Cinders is comforted by her guardian angel, Practice; Prince Charming shows his own ballet shoes, and the three ladies are not all of them what they seem

123 The Open Window, and the Lake District Challenge

124 Eileen Walters ('Patience') and the Brotherhood altar in London. The gold curtains, bought as 'the best' by Radiance, still have some use today!

125 Ylana and Colum come down from the platform; the fireplace is stone and 'Arts and Crafts'; Anne and Monique lived in Richmond

126 Main chapel picture taken professionally for a celebratory brochure; 'Pearl' Satchell became Mrs Rauberts; Gefry Horrabbin (Sun Ray)

127 Joan, Eunice. Margot Kemhadjian was 'Pearl' in the Brotherhood

128 Ruby Jewel, from a Brotherhood album; HULLO SUN

129 Astrology School Council; the table is perfect for such meetings

130 IN WEST AFRICA. Top (in Port Harcourt), rear: John Okonkwo, Fred Bote-Kwame, Simon Emelogwu; front: Hamida, Sunday John Enyia, Temple Amachree, Joseph Jaja, George Jaja. Below left: Fred, Hector George, Jones Babalola, John Okonkwo, Tamanoemi and Temple Amachree. Bottom right Fred with Prosper Agbenkey

131 Wedding of Fred & Hamida; Britta Hudig ('White Star') initiated 1969

132 Two retreats in Denmark; Annemarie Libera ('Red Rose') and Johannes Rankl ('Shining Knight')

133 Temple gathering, early 1990s; opening of Star Centre at Limburg, South Netherlands, May 2005

134 Commins family, mid-1990s; Surrey BC is a suburb of Vancouver

135 Geoffrey, Melanie ('Francesca'), Ylana, Jenny

136 Geoffrey Dent, Brother Alban   137 Stuart Neil, Brother Stuart

138 The Garden of Communion has quickly become much loved – and so has the Americas Retreat Center

139 Dents and Codys, with just Geoffrey missing; David Repard of the CHO

140 Sandor is Hungarian by birth, and has been of great help to Bela Balogh, Brother John, in establishing the work there

141 Morgan Hesmondhalgh and Peter James would both insist they were only part of a big and willing team!

142 THE LIGHT BRINGER – deliberately our publication for the Millennium. Malcolm White drives the mini-tractor, a stalwart of the camps. He and Roslyn are also to be seen in the Avebury group, p. 100

143 Kathryn Bingham has proved herself central to all our work with children

144 Cape Town picture from Jenny's visit in 2007. Maybelle van Warmelo, South African leader; Evelyn Addy, Accra group leader, visiting South Africa; Evelyn van Vloten, Kloof (Natal) group leader until she passed

145 Anne Cornock-Taylor, Sister Diana;Monique, Sister White Rose; the arrangement may as well be Anne's as Monique's, so closely did they work

146 With their back to us, the healers are Madeleine Allum, Joan Punchard, John Brereton, and Kathleen Pepper

147 The sitters include Colin and Jo Blencowe, old 'Eaglets', and Hazel Wilkinson ('Christine', 'Christopher' and 'Unity')

148 Among faces not noted elsewhere are Pat Harrison (Canada 'Mother'), Trustee Roger Earis (back, centre) and Esther Eichelberger ('White Rose') from Minnesota, USA. David and Jo are 'Truth' and 'Steadfast'

149 Jane Sorbi, Sister Starlight, stands with Denise Badmington ('Golden Rose')

150 Doris Commins and Gay Robinson

151 In good weather at the 2008 Conference, a number of very constructive meetings were held outside; John LeFevre, at around 90

152 The 'Grandmother' and 'Mother' ceremonies were witnessed by Jack Sorbi ('Shining Knight') and Simon Bentley ('Christopher');Ylana

153 Jenny Dent